Paper Flowers

Valerie Janitch

Chilton Book Company
Radnor, Pennsylvania

© Valerie Janitch 1976

All rights reserved   First Edition
Published in 1977 by Chilton Book Company, Radnor, Pennsylvania
Published simultaneously in Canada by Thomas Nelson & Sons, Ltd.

Library of Congress Cataloging in Publication Data

Janitch, Valerie.
  Paper Flowers

  (Chilton's creative crafts series)
  1. Paper Flowers. I. Title.
TT892.J36   745.59'43   76-11006
ISBN 0-8019-6414-8
ISBN 0-8019-6415-6 pbk.

Printed and bound in Spain
First published in Great Britain by Ward Lock Limited, London

Note : If any of the materials listed are
unfamiliar to you, just check
the glossary for detailed
descriptions.

Contents

Preface	5	Presentation Why this book is different
Materials and Equipment	6	Crêpe paper, Duplex paper, soft-ply tissue, plain tissue paper Wires and stems Adhesives Equipment Easy measuring, metric conversions
The Special Techniques	8	Cupping, frilling, stroking, curling
The Basic Methods	8	Templates, Flowers and stems, Leaves
Buttercups and Daisies	12	Wild flowers for any time of the year
Daffodils, Narcissi and Gentians	15	Harbingers of spring
Japanese and St Brigid Anemones	22	A study in contrasts
Marigolds, Marigolds	26	A sunburst of colour
Morning Glory and a Posy of Moss Roses	30	A romantic, old-world theme
Love-in-a-Mist and Carnations	37	Perfect for a party table
Asters and Tiger Lilies	41	Two jewel-coloured favourites
Canterbury Bells and Ranunculus	49	Country flowers come to town
Petunias and Pincushions	53	Familiar and contrasting garden flowers
Poppies and Cornflowers	59	From the old-fashioned wheat field
Roses All The Way	63	Three beautiful, contrasting styles
Sunflower and Peonies	76	Giant decorations with sensational impact
Dahlias and Chrysanthemums	83	Richly-glowing golden colours
Helleborus Niger: Christmas Rose and Ivy Trails	86	The Christmas rose in two guises

Kitchenalia Floribunda 91 Sheer fun with everyday materials

Moonbeam Icicalia 93 An ethereal, fantasy bouquet

What To Use and Where To Find It 95

Index 96

Preface

My mother has green fingers. And if that's not enough – she talks to her plants, too. Sadly, I didn't inherit her talents so I stay indoors and make *my* flowers in paper.

Paper flowers don't compete with the garden variety, which are much too beautiful to imitate. But they do have an extrovert charm of their own; they're bright and gay and cheerful and decorative. They're always in season and they last almost indefinitely. They don't wilt in central heating and they don't need water. Even the most exotic blooms are not expensive; and you don't waste money on fertilisers, weed killers, miracle-feeds, pest repellents or greenhouses. And there's also the pleasure and satisfaction of creating them.

Just remember – they must never be mistaken for 'real'. If they are, you will have failed. Paper flowers *must* look what they are: unashamedly fake, stunningly magnificent and quite a bit larger than life!

Presentation

You can forget vases were ever invented and re-think all your previous ideas about flower-arranging. Leave a posy lying casually on a polished table or pin single flower-heads between the folds of plain curtains for a party; tuck them into the frame of a mirror or behind pictures, twine stems round a wrought iron lamp bracket, trail long sprays across a wall or along a window-ledge, encircle the base of an iced celebration cake. Have them peeping over the edge of a lidded wicker basket, filling an empty fireplace or spilling out of a disused coal scuttle. Imagination is all you need.

Why This Book Is Different – and How It Works

Paper flowers are fun and this book sets out to prove it. At least half the fun is the surprising speed with which you produce a spectacular creation, opening the book at any design and snipping straight into your first flower.

The book is so arranged that it can be used in two different ways; for those who like to study the theory and gain background knowledge before they begin, or for people impatient to start work, who prefer to learn as they go along. So choose your own method to suit your personality!

Of course it helps to know the best tools to use and the types and properties of the papers and other materials employed for the flowers, but you can get along quite happily if you haven't time to study everything in detail before you begin.

You will find the directions clearly set out and easy to follow, with plenty of diagrams for visual guidance, so you can be sure of results which are not only creatively satisfying but, above all, *fun*!

Materials and Equipment

Artificial flowers are becoming so popular that many craft shops are stocking a growing range of interesting accessories like stamens, centres, leaves and so on. Nevertheless, paper flower making often tends to be a spontaneous, spur-of-the-moment activity, so I have avoided using any of those specialised refinements, in case you have difficulty in obtaining them. Instead, I have used the same types of readily available papers, wire and other items for the majority of the flowers; everything mentioned in the lists of materials can be found in craft shops, stationers, Woolworth's or hardware stores.

You can make flowers from tissue paper, cartridge or construction paper, wrapping paper, kitchen foil, face tissues or even toilet paper! But for sheer versatility, for depth and subtlety of colour, and, most of all for its unique quality of 'stretching', you can't beat crêpe! All this adds up to a really bold effect, which is why I have concentrated on this one type of paper.

Crêpe paper: Always buy good quality crêpe paper. Inferior crêpes have less 'stretch' and they tear easily when you *do* try to stretch them. The secret of the stretch lies in the *grain* of the paper, and it is important to understand how to recognise and use this. If you examine the paper, you will see that the surface is covered with tiny lines (or indentations), all running in the same direction: this is the grain. If you pull the paper gently in the same direction as the lines, nothing happens; but if you pull it the other way – *across* the lines – it will stretch. Always remember that the arrows on a pattern or diagram indicate the direction of the grain: it is essential to follow this when cutting your crêpe.

Crêpe paper does have a *right and wrong side*. By studying the surface closely, you will see that one side has a dull, matt finish: this is the *right* side. The difference is usually more apparent on dark colours than lighter shades. When the difference is obvious, use the right side for the upper surface of petals and leaves.

Duplex crêpe paper: This 'luxury' double crêpe is, in fact, two layers of single crêpe bonded together – usually a pale colour on one side and a deeper shade on the reverse. Unfortunately, Duplex is not easy to obtain everywhere, though it can be ordered by mail, and is about twice the price of ordinary crêpe. However, a little goes a long way, especially if you cut it economically.

Soft-ply tissue: This term covers absorbent face tissues; paper hankies; soft toilet paper; soft, two-, three- or even four-ply paper table napkins, and so on. All these come in a wide range of colours, which can often be useful in the construction of a flower. Strips of twin-ply face tissue make excellent padding.

Plain tissue paper: This is single thickness, very thin, but smooth and firm, and creases easily. For craftwork, it comes in an attractive range of colours. Although it can be substituted for soft-ply tissue to cover a flower-centre, it is not suitable for padding.

Wires – and stems: For the stems of most medium-sized flowers, I use plastic-covered garden wire: but any medium-gauge flexible galvanised wire would be just as suitable.

When a lighter weight is needed, I have used a *fine soft wire* which is sold for general household purposes and occasionally, a *very fine wire* – either finest florists' or rose wire.

If the head of the flower is too big and heavy, the wire stem will bend and droop. In such cases, I generally make the flower up on a wire foundation, but with only a short stem, which is then fixed to a thin garden cane for support. Place the cane alongside the wire and attach by binding with tape (or a narrow strip of crêpe) at the top, mid-way and the base. This, of course, means the flower will have an absolutely straight, rigid stem, but the head itself can be angled by leaving just enough wire between the base of the flower and the top of the stick to form a flexible hinge.

Adhesives

A flexible rubber cement – often described as 'fabric adhesive' – is ideal for paper. But it will not stick non-porous materials like metal, glass, plastic, etcetera: for these you will need an all-purpose clear adhesive.

Fabric adhesive (rubber cement) is usually sold in tubes (with a small spatula for spreading) and jars (with a built-in brush). A tube is essential, for tiny applications: but ideally, have a jar as well – to deal with large surfaces.

All-purpose clear adhesive comes in a tube, usually with a long, narrow, pointed nozzle – with which you can apply the solution direct: or, for very tiny surfaces, use the head of a pin.

Wallpaper paste or transparent paper paste is useful for stiffening, but is too wet for sticking crêpe. Mix a bare teaspoonful of powder with cold water in a small basin or yoghurt carton. Although it is rather extravagant for general use, a **dry solid** stick adhesive is the perfect answer when you want to bond two pieces of crêpe paper together to make a double thickness, or to combine two shades to simulate a Duplex crêpe. The adhesive comes in a small cylindrical container, and twists up, like a lipstick: raise the stick so that only just enough emerge for use, otherwise it may break off at the base.

In no circumstances use any of the older types of glue which darken and become hard and brittle on drying. These are likely to ruin your work.

Equipment

The essential tools for the job are few, and generally to be found in the average home. Two pairs of *scissors* – one large, the other small and pointed – will be in constant use, and you will find it pays dividends to keep them sharp and well-aligned. A pair of *wire cutters* will prevent the temptation to ruin your scissors! A *pencil* with a good point, a *ruler* and *eraser* are the other basic necessities with, for many of the designs, a pair of *compasses*. *Pinking shears* are occasionally called for, to create a special effect, but are not essential. A *craft knife* is sometimes useful and a *set-square* can be an asset.

You will also need *tracing or ordinary household greaseproof paper*, with *stiff paper or thin card* to make your patterns. *Sewing thread, paper clips, pins*, etcetera, will be wanted now and then, as will a *fine knitting needle, cocktail or manicure stick*, a fairly *fine paint-brush* and a roll of *adhesive tape* (preferably matt-surface transparent mending tape).

A well-organised and tidy working area is worth striving for in any craft-work! But it's particularly helpful in paper flower making, especially for mass-production, when I find a selection of small, empty *yoghurt or cream cartons* (or paper cups) and larger plastic *ice cream or similar containers*, very handy to protect the prepared parts and keep them separate.

Easy Measuring – Metric Conversions

Don't be confused if these tend to differ. This is done to give you the nearest *practical* working measurement, rather than an accurate but unnecessarily fiddly conversion.

The Special Techniques

the magic touches which make a paper flower

The secret of successful paper flowers lies in the various basic techniques which transform flat paper – especially crêpe – into the delicate curves and rounded shapes of natural petals and leaves. Practice first on odd pieces of paper, to get the 'feel' of how to do it. For some of the techniques it is important to understand the unusual properties of crêpe paper – especially the grain: this is fully explained on page 6.

Cupping: Hold the crêpe petal (or leaf or sepal) in both hands: place your thumbs in the centre, and gently stretch the paper to form a curved 'cup'. You can also create a 'domed' shape by cupping the lower half of the petal in this way, then turning it over and cupping the upper half from the back.

Frilling: As with cupping, this applies to crêpe paper only. Gently stretch the cut edge of the paper (which must be cut at right angles *across* the grain) between the fingertips, to form a frill.

Stroking: This treatment applies to almost any kind of paper as long as it is strong enough: face tissue, for instance, would tear. Crêpe responds very well, but only if stroked *along* the grain (see below).

If you are right-handed, hold the top end in your left hand, and gently draw the paper smoothly between your right thumb and the blade of your scissors or a blunt knife, held in the same hand. Repeat until you have the amount of 'curl' required. Heavier papers need firmer stroking, but always begin gently, and you will soon gauge how much more strength is needed.

Curling: Crêpe paper can be curled by stroking, as above, *only* if you want the curl to follow the line of the grain. To curl crêpe across the grain, either horizontally or diagonally, place a fine knitting needle, cocktail or manicure stick, on the paper, close to the edge, at the angle indicated by a broken line on the appropriate pattern. Then roll the paper smoothly and tightly round the stick, using the fingertips. Extract the needle or stick and allow the curl to open out slightly. This technique is mainly characteristic of rose petals – see the patterns on pages 64, 72 and 75.

Note: If you are stroking or re-cupping petals on a finished flower, always begin with the outer ones and work inwards towards the centre.

The Basic Methods

all you need to know plus some useful tips

Templates: To cut petals, leaves, and so on, you will often need to make a template. Trace the pattern on to tracing or household greaseproof paper. Turn the paper over and rub over the lines on the *back* with a soft lead pencil. Turn the tracing over again and place it on a piece of thin card or stiff paper. Hold it firmly down to prevent any movement, and go over the lines once more, this time with a hard pencil or ball point pen, to transfer the outline to the paper or card beneath. Cut the shape out and indicate the name and part of the flower on it, together with any arrows and other markings. Keep your templates carefully, as they can be used over and over again.

Cutting petals and leaves: Place the template on the paper, remembering that in the case of crêpe the arrows must always follow the direction of the grain. Practice holding or fixing the template in position, and then cutting round it. Try to avoid drawing a pencil outline on the paper, as it may show in the finished flower. If you do prefer to draw the shape, cut just inside the pencil line. Similarly, with any ruled line which may show on the finished flower either cut just inside it, or erase it before making up.

You can save a lot of time by folding your paper concertina-wise and cutting out several petals or leaf shapes together. Grip the paper with spring- or paper-clips while cutting out, to stop the layers shifting.

Cutting double petals and leaves: Always cut the two pieces of crêpe together, so that they are identical. Place the wrong sides of the paper together, clip the two pieces together, if necessary, position your template on top and cut round it. Keep the two pieces together to prevent the pairs becoming muddled before being stuck together. You can, of course, fold several double layers of paper to cut a number of petals together.

Making up double petals and leaves: As crêpe stretches out of shape when damp, I find the safest and easiest way to bond two layers of crêpe paper together is a *dry solid stick adhesive*. Holding the underneath half of the petal or leaf firmly down on a flat surface, working along the grain to avoid pulling the paper out of shape, draw a thin film of adhesive over the paper: then lower the top piece gently into position, beginning at the tip and smoothing it down, lifting to re-adjust if necessary. Trim the edges neatly.

However, if you prefer to use your *fabric adhesive or rubber cement* for this purpose, apply it very sparingly, just smearing a mere film round the outside before quickly pressing the two sides of the petal together.

Making a folded fringe: Follow the individual directions for cutting your strip of paper to size and folding it across the grain, as indicated by the broken line, right side inside. Snip the folded edge as indicated, to the depth stated and shown on the appropriate diagram: then open out the paper, smoothing it quite flat and place it on the table, right side down. Lay a ruler on top, one edge against the fold-line; lift the uncovered side of the paper and re-fold it over the ruler along the previous fold-line, but in the opposite direction, of course. Press the fold lightly over the ruler before removing it, but *do not re-crease*; just let the paper curve round instead of making a sharp fold. Finally, lightly glue the cut edges together (often indicated by x's on the diagram), to hold the fringe in shape.

Speedy fringe-snipping: If you have only one strip of fringe to prepare, fold the paper across the grain in the usual way: then fold it in half *along* the grain – and then again, keeping the long, crosswise folded edge absolutely level, so that you can snip through the four double thicknesses together.

If you have several strips of fringe to prepare, fold each piece across the grain first, and grip the lower edges firmly together with spring or paper clips. Keep all the folded edges level and snip through all the thicknesses.

Flowers and Stems

Fixing fringe and petals in position: Apply fabric adhesive (rubber cement) to the base of single petals, or spread along the lower edge of strips, a short section at a time.

When wrapping strips of centre fringe, petals or foliage round and round the centre of a flower, it is very important to keep the lower edges of successive rounds absolutely level with the previous ones unless otherwise directed; as you add more layers, there is a tendency to slip down. If you find this happening, ease gently up before they become firmly stuck.

Always begin a new strip where the last one finished. This will ensure an even thickness of layers all round the flower.

INTRODUCTION:
BINDING TIPS OF STALKS

1

2

3

4

5

6

7

Covering centres: To secure the edge of a paper circle covering the padded centre of a flower, use either sewing thread or fine wire to bind it tightly round the stem, close underneath the padding.

Binding: Cut a long, narrow strip of crêpe – about ½ inch or 10 mm wide, unless otherwise directed – *across* the grain of the paper, so that the grain runs from side to side. I always cut several ½ inch (10 mm) 'slices' off one end of a folded new roll of green crêpe, to keep in reserve. Begin binding close under the petals or sepals, glueing round the base of the flower. Continue twisting the paper at a slight angle down the stem, stretching it smoothly as you go and glueing neatly at the bottom.

Binding the tips of stalks: To make a smoothly *rounded tip*, cut the binding straight across the end, and spread a little adhesive close to the end (diagram 1): place the wire on the adhesive – as diagram 1, the tip a short distance from the corner. Turn this corner over (diagram 2) – then fold the other corner over, as diagram 3. Now bind down the stalk in the usual way (diagram 4).

For a *pointed tip*, cut the binding diagonally across the grain, and spread a little adhesive close to the end (diagram 5): place the wire parallel with, and close to, the diagonal cut – as diagram 5. Roll the paper smoothly round with the fingertips (diagram 6), then continue binding down the stalk in the usual way (diagram 7).

Padding: Many flowers are padded with strips of two-ply soft tissue. To pad underneath the centre of a flower, and build up a rounded base, cut strips about 9 inches (23 cm) long by 1 inch (25 mm) wide. Make these narrower if only a little is needed or wider if you are padding an unusually large area. Spread a generous trail of adhesive along one half of a strip (diagram 1): then fold it in half lenthways, adhesive inside (diagram 2). Spread adhesive liberally over the base of the flower, then wrap the strip around the top of the stem, pushing well up underneath the centre and pressing smoothly into position, adding more adhesive if necessary. Build up the shape with more strips, as required. Cotton wool may also be used to pad the base of a flower: mould it into shape with fabric adhesive or rubber cement.

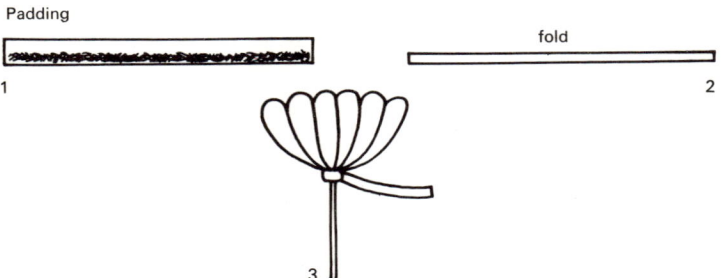

Padding stems: Cut strips of twin-ply face tissue about 9 inches (23 cm) by 1 inch (25 mm): fold in half lengthways, as above – but *without* any adhesive inside. Glue at the top, and then bind down the stem as for crêpe – but with the folded edge of the strip uppermost.

Colouring crêpe: A hint of shading on petals can be very effective, and so can a brilliant streak of contrasting colour; I use either oil pastels or waterproof drawing inks.

For *shadows*, moisten a piece of cotton wool or face tissue with a little ink (diluted with water, if necessary) and dab it on a scrap of waste paper until it is almost dry. Then gently smooth it over the surface of the crêpe, continuing with further applications until you achieve the required colour. For a grainy texture, rub the surface of the crêpe lightly with an oil pastel.

For *streaks of colour*, use a fine, pointed water-colour brush and just enough ink to make a bold slash of colour without making the paper wet. Work quickly and confidently, flicking the brush lightly over the surface of the crêpe.

'Water-painting' crêpe: Not only does wetting crêpe cause it to stretch, wrinkle and tear, it also makes the colour run alarmingly! However, with care and caution, you can use these features to create some quite exciting effects. An example of this is demonstrated by the French marigolds on page 26.

Leaves
the all-important finishing touch

Attaching the leaves to their stalks: Measure the leaf against the bound stalk, with the tip of the leaf just above the top of the stalk, and mark the stalk at the base of the leaf. Spread a trail of adhesive along the stalk, then press the leaf down over it and pinch firmly together so that the shape of the stalk shows down the centre on the front of the leaf.

Jagged edges: Some leaves must be cut with a jagged or serrated edge and this is specially effective in Duplex or double crêpe. Jagged edges are quite easily achieved by adopting a sort of hiccupping action as you cut!

Holding the template firmly against the paper, begin at the tip of the leaf – A – and make a short, slightly curved cut, as the arrow in diagram 1, stopping against the edge of the template. Then 'hiccup', pulling the scissors back a fraction – and make another, similar, cut as diagram 2. Hiccup backwards again – and cut again – as diagram 3. Continue round to the centre at the base – B. Now turn the paper over and hold the template against the back – fitted against the previously cut edge (diagram 4) – and, beginning again at A, cut the other side in the same way.

INTRODUCTION:
Leaves: Jagged Edges

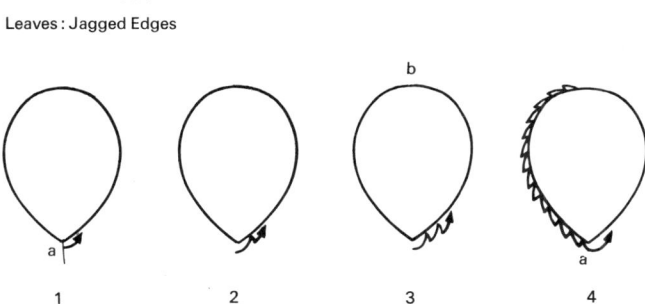

Veins: It can often improve a crêpe leaf if you mark the veins. To do this, place the leaf face down on a slightly padded surface, and use the point of a knitting needle, or a cocktail or manicure stick, to 'draw' the central and radiating veins on the back.

Buttercups & Daisies

These several-times-larger-than-life wild-flowers bring a welcome splash of sunshine to a dark corner at any time of the year.

Field Buttercups

Materials: *Buttercup yellow crêpe paper for petals*
Primrose yellow crêpe paper for stamens
Olive green crêpe paper for sepals, stem and leaves
Lime green soft-ply tissue (or substitute) for centre
Plastic-covered garden wire
Sewing thread or fine wire
Cotton wool
Solid stick adhesive (optional)
Fabric adhesive or rubber cement

Stem and centre: Cut a 12 inch (30 cm) length of garden wire. Turn over $\frac{3}{8}$ inch (10 mm) at one end, then wrap and glue cotton wool around it to form a round ball about $\frac{1}{2}$ inch (12 mm) in diameter. Cut a $2\frac{1}{2}$ inch (6·5 cm) diameter circle of lime green tissue, place the centre over the top of the cotton wool ball, draw the edges down smoothly; bind tightly underneath with thread or wire.

Cut a piece of primrose yellow crêpe paper – grain as arrows, diagram 1. Make a folded fringe strip (page 9) as diagram 2, snipping the folded edge very finely to a depth of about 1 inch (25 mm). Glue the yellow strip round underneath the centre, keeping the cut edges of the yellow and green level.
Petals: Trace the pattern and make a template (page 8). Cut five double petals (page 9) in buttercup yellow crêpe, and make up as described on page 8. Cup the centre of each petal (page 8). Then glue them evenly round the centre, lower edges level.
Sepals: Make a template, and cut five in green crêpe. Glue each directly

behind a petal. Glue a little cotton wool underneath the centre, to round off the base. Then bind the base and stem as directed on page 10.

Cup the *underside* of each sepal, then pull it down and stroke the tip (page 8) to curl up, as illustrated. Re-cup the petals, if necessary. Then lightly glue the undersides of each pair where they meet, as x's on the pattern.

Leaves: Make a template, cut twice in green crêpe, and glue the base of each round the stem, directly opposite one another.

Bud: Cut a 10 inch (25 cm) length of garden wire, turn over the end and wrap cotton wool around it as for the flower centre, but to measure about 1½ inches (35 mm) in diameter. Cut a 5 inch (13 cm) diameter circle of buttercup yellow crêpe. Place the centre over the cotton wool ball, draw the sides down smoothly and evenly twist and glue the edge round the wire as diagram 3.

Sepals: Cut five in green crêpe. Cup the lower half of each on the *wrong* side. Then glue them evenly round the base of the bud, positioning so that the tips meet centrally on top. Stroke the upper half of each sepal to curl round over the top, as illustrated, before fixing lightly with adhesive to the side of the bud, to hold in position. Bind the base and stem as before.

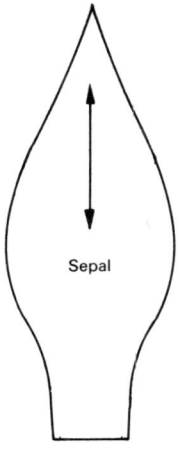
Sepal

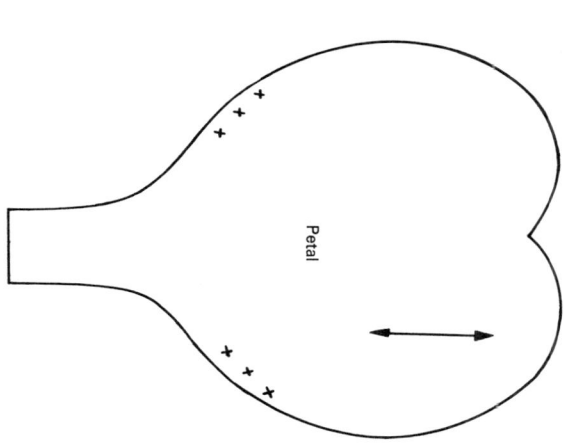
Petal

Leaf

Meadow Daisies

Materials: White crêpe paper for top petals
               Pale pink crêpe paper for under petals
               Deep yellow crêpe paper for centre
               Light green crêpe paper for centre
               Olive green crêpe paper for stem
               Light green soft-ply tissue (or substitute) for centre
               Plastic-covered garden wire
               Sewing thread or fine wire
               Cotton wool
               Fabric adhesive or rubber cement

Stem and centre: Cut a 12 inch (30 cm) length of garden wire, turn over ¼ inch (5 mm) at one end, then wrap and glue cotton wool around it to form a round ball about ⅜ inch (10 mm) in diameter.

Cut a 2½ inch (6·5 cm) diameter circle of light green tissue, place the centre over the top of the cotton wool ball, draw the edge down smoothly all round and bind tightly underneath with thread or wire.

Cut two pieces of crêpe paper, one in deep yellow and the other light green, with the grain as arrowed in diagram 1. Make a folded fringe strip (page 9) as diagram 2, snipping the folded edge closely to a depth of about ⅜ inch (10 mm). Then glue the two strips together along the lower edge – fringed top edges absolutely level.

With the green side inside and the snipped top edge exactly level with the covered centre, glue this double strip round underneath the centre, keeping the lower edge level.

Cut another piece of deep yellow crêpe the same depth, but 12 inches (30 cm) wide. Prepare in the same way as the first two strips, then glue it round over the double strip. If the centre rides up, pull it firmly down, spread adhesive underneath the flower, pinch together and allow to dry.

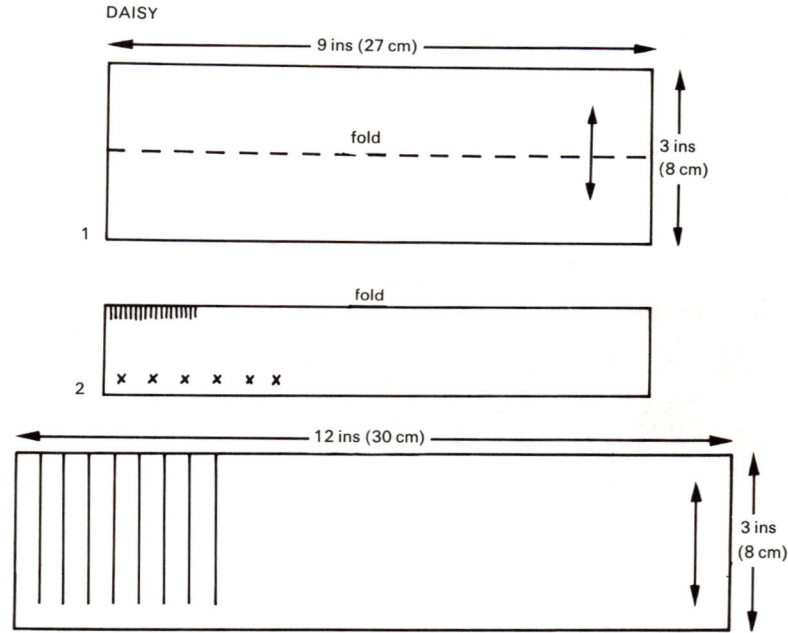

DAISY

Petals: Cut two pieces of white crêpe with the grain as arrowed in diagram 3. Cut these at ½ inch (10 mm) intervals, to within ½ inch (10 mm) of the lower edge as indicated on the diagram. Then snip off the top corners of each petal (diagram 4). Glue these two pieces together along the lower edge, positioning so that each cut on the upper strip falls over the centre of a petal underneath. Now glue round the base of the flower, placing the lower edge of the petals ½ inch (10 mm) above the lower edge of the previous yellow strip. Circle the centre three times, marking the lower edge equally into three and glueing one section at a time.

Cut two pieces of pale pink crêpe 3 inches (8 cm) deep, but only 4 inches (10 cm) wide. Prepare these as the white petals, then glue round the flower.

Using adhesive, fix a little cotton wool underneath the centre to round off the base. Then bind the base and stem as directed on page 10. Stroke the petals gently (page 8) to curl them round as illustrated.

Daffodils, Narcissi & Gentians

Harbingers of spring, daffodils and narcissi arrive early to herald the first bright sunshine. In contrast, the deep blue gentian flowers profusely throughout the summer, growing in tight clumps on the stony ground it loves.

Trumpet Daffodils

Materials: Primrose yellow crêpe paper for petals
Buttercup yellow crêpe paper for trumpet
Brown crêpe paper for bud case
Olive green crêpe paper for stem and leaf
Lime green soft-ply tissue (or plain tissue or crêpe) for centre
Plastic-covered garden wire
Solid stick adhesive (optional)
Fabric adhesive or rubber cement

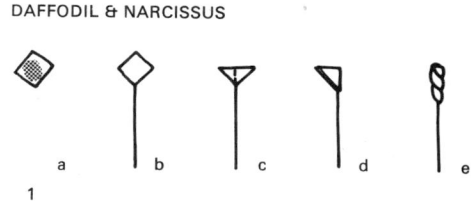

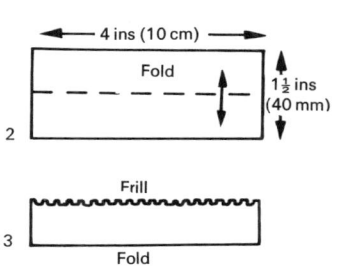

Stem and centre: Cut a 12 inch (30 cm) length of garden wire, and twist a 1 inch (25 mm) square of lime green tissue round one end, as diagram 1. Spread adhesive from the centre of the paper to one corner (diagram 1a): lay the tip of the wire in it (diagram 1b): fold the upper half diagonally over (diagram 1c): fold the right-hand half over to the left-hand side and glue (diagram 1d): then twist and glue round the wire (diagram 1e).

Cut a piece of primrose yellow crêpe paper with grain as arrowed (diagram 2). Fold in half, as indicated, then frill the cut edges (see page 8), as diagram 3. Glue round the centre, the yellow frilled edge level with the green-covered tip of the stem.

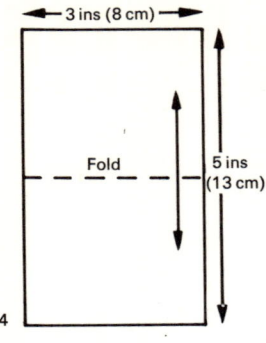

4

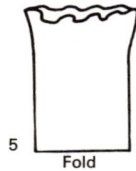

5

6

Trumpet: Cut a piece of buttercup yellow crêpe with grain as arrowed (diagram 4). Fold in half, as indicated, trim the cut edges absolutely level and curve round to form a cylinder, overlapping the side edges and joining all four layers with adhesive. Frill the top (cut) edges as diagram 5.

Gathering the folded edge tightly with the fingertips of your left hand, press your right forefinger down inside and round out the base as diagram 6, to form a bell shape. Allow the lower edge to open out, spread adhesive behind the gathers, then carefully lower the stem through the trumpet until the lower edges of the trumpet and yellow centre are level. Re-gather, and press tightly to stick. Re-shape the trumpet.

Petals: Trace the pattern and make a template (page 8). Cut six *double* petals in primrose yellow crêpe (page 9), and make up as described on page 9.

Spread a very little adhesive down the right-hand side of one petal, as shown by the shaded section in diagram 7, and glue a second petal so that it overlaps the first as shown. Continue in the same way until all six petals are joined. Glue the first and last petal together, overlapping as before.

Spread adhesive all round the base of the trumpet. Then slide the circle of petals up the stem, until the lower edges of the petals and trumpet are level: press firmly together. Bind the base and stem as directed on page 10.

Bud case: Make a template, cut once in brown crêpe, and glue round the stem behind the flower head, as illustrated.

Leaf: Cut a leaf in green crêpe 9 inches (23 cm) long by ⅝ inch (15 mm) at its widest point (grain running lengthways) – tapering to a point at the top (diagram 8). Spread adhesive over the base and wrap round the stem, so that it stands up alongside it.

Cup the *back* of each petal (page 8), so that they curve round and back as illustrated. Bend the stem just behind the bud case, to turn the head sideways.

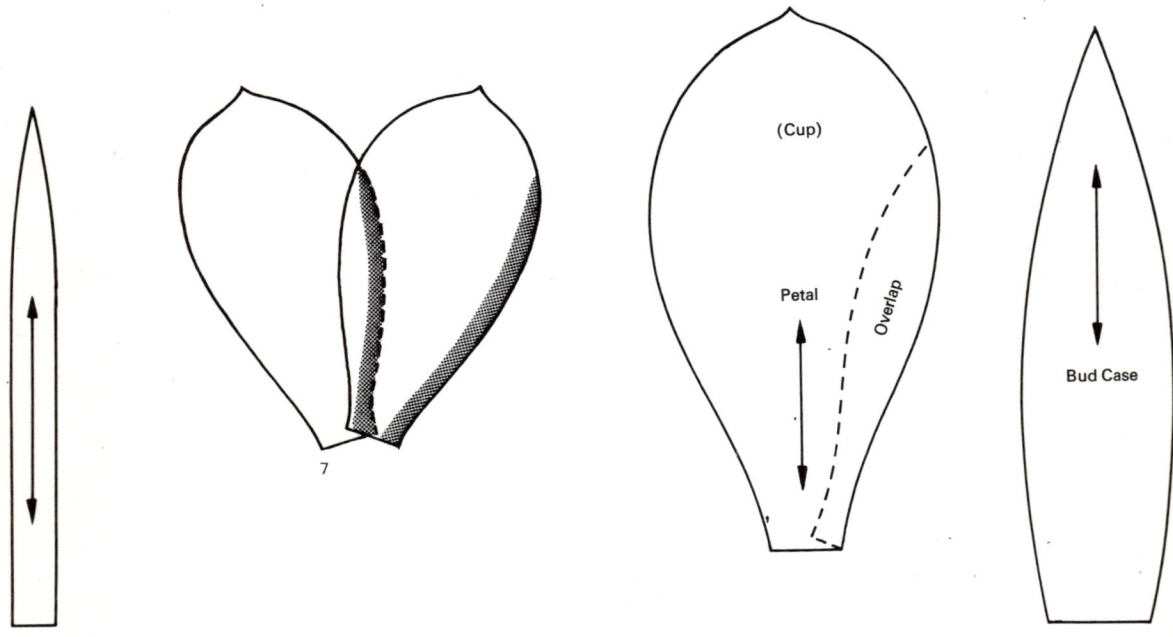

Buttercups and Daisies (pages 12 and 13)

Poet's Narcissi

If you haven't any ink, use water-colour or a felt pen to create the striking centre of the pheasant's eye or poet's narcissus.

Materials: Primrose yellow crêpe paper for centre
White crêpe paper for petals
Orange crêpe paper for trumpet
Brown crêpe paper for bud case
Olive green crêpe paper for stem and leaf
Lime green soft-ply tissue (or substitute) for centre
Plastic-covered garden wire
Scarlet drawing ink (or substitute)
Solid stick adhesive (optional)
Fabric adhesive or rubber cement

Follow the directions for the daffodil, substituting white crêpe paper for the petals – and making the trumpet as follows.

Trumpet: Cut a piece of orange crêpe, with the grain as arrowed (diagram 9). Fold in half, as indicated; trim the cut edges absolutely level and curve round to form a cylinder, overlapping the side edges and glueing all four layers to join (use adhesive sparingly). Dip a paint-brush into the scarlet ink, then gently touch the cut edges until a little ink is absorbed, and the paper forms a crinkly frill. Allow the trumpet to dry thoroughly – then shape the base and complete the narcissus as the daffodil.

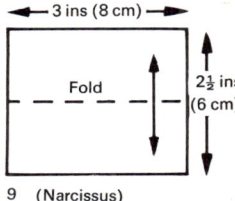

9 (Narcissus)

Mountain Gentians

Materials: Deep blue crêpe paper for petals
White crêpe paper for stamens
Light green crêpe paper for centre
Olive green crêpe paper for sepals, stem and leaves
Plastic-covered garden wire
Cotton wool
Sewing thread
Fabric adhesive or rubber cement

Stem and centre: Cut an 8 inch (20 cm) length of garden wire. Then cut a strip of light green crêpe paper 1 inch (25 mm) long by ⅛ inch (3 mm) wide with grain running lengthways; fold it in half – across the grain. Squeeze a little adhesive on to the tip of the stem, insert between the cut ends of the paper, and press together (diagram 1). Wrap and glue cotton wool around the stem, covering 1 inch (25 mm) immediately below the paper strip. Make the padding about ⅜ inch (10 mm) in diameter at the widest point, tapering off to nothing above and below (diagram 2).

Cut a 1½ inch (40 mm) diameter circle of light green crêpe. Cup the centre (page 8), then place the padded stem on top, slightly to the right of the centre, as diagram 3 (grain as arrows). Spread a little adhesive round the edge

Daffodils, Narcissi and Gentians (pages 15 and 19)

of the circle, as shown by the shaded section, then wrap the right half of the circle smoothly round, the top edge of the paper level with the tip of the wire inside the strip. Spread adhesive round the left edge of the circle, between x's on diagram 3, and bring this smoothly round over the other side. Finish off neatly, gathering and glueing the excess paper underneath (diagram 4): as long as the upper half is smoothly covered, it won't matter if the lower part is untidy.

Trim the strip at the top to a rounded point, as diagram 4.

GENTIAN

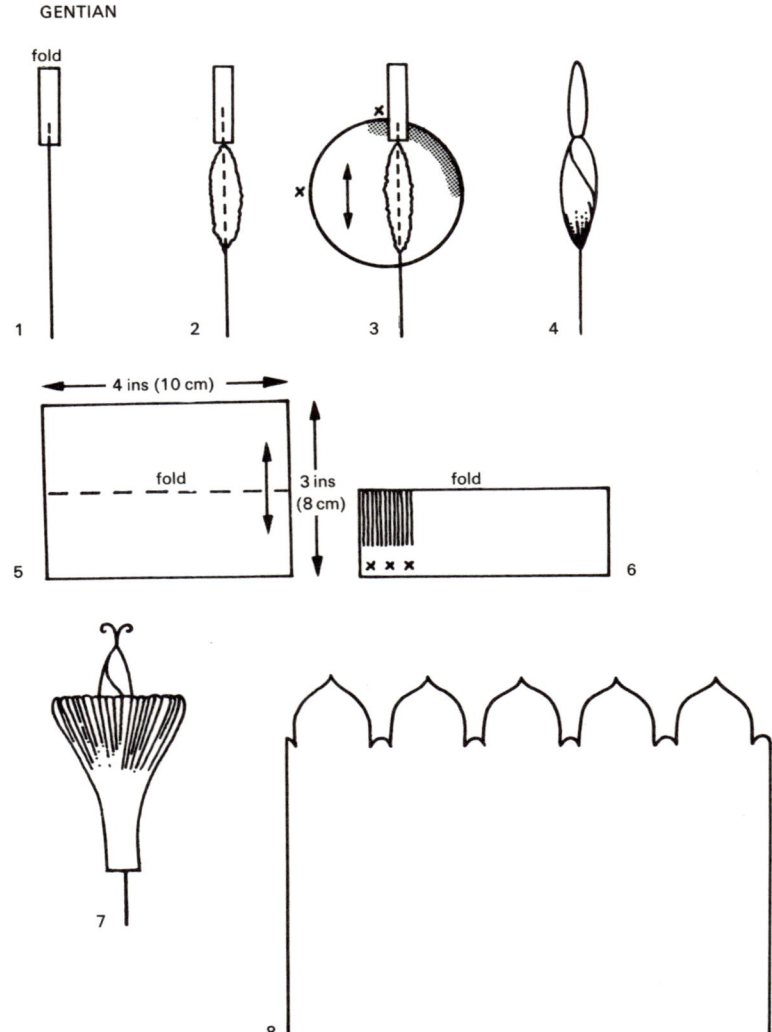

Cut a piece of white crêpe with the grain as arrowed (diagram 5). Make a folded fringe strip (page 9) as diagram 6, snipping the folded edge very closely to a depth of half-way.

Glue the white strip round the base of the centre, so that the fringed top edge reaches half-way up, level with the widest point (diagram 7).

Divide and stroke (page 8) the two halves of the pointed strip at the top, to curl round as in diagram 7.

Petals: Trace the pattern (ignoring the broken line) and make a template (page 8). Fold a piece of blue crêpe concertina-wise, the width of the pattern (grain as arrows), and cut five petals *plus* an overlap at one edge as indicated

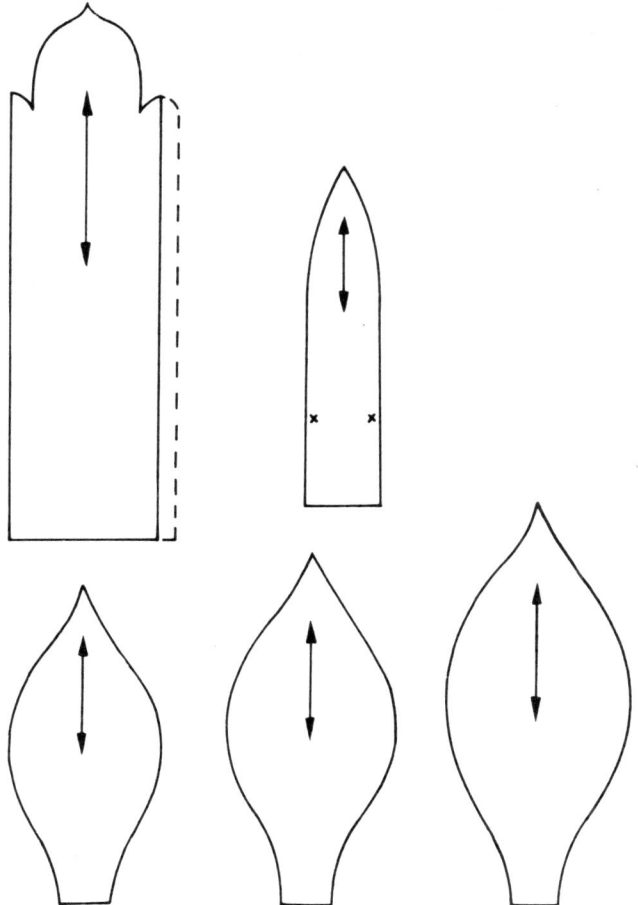

by the broken line, so that when opened out, the paper looks like diagram 8. Curve round and stick the side edges, matching the overlap neatly (use adhesive sparingly).

Thread a needle and gather just above the straight edge. Draw up the gathers and press down inside with your forefinger to 'bell' out the base slightly (as for the daffodil trumpet). Now open the gathers to lower the stem down through the petals: spread adhesive round the base of the centre, then draw up the gathers evenly round it and press firmly together.

Sepals: Make a template. Fold a piece of olive green crêpe as for the petals, and cut five sepals – slitting the fold to x between each pair. Glue the base round over the petals, lower edges level, so that a sepal falls behind each tall petal.

Bind the base and stem as directed on page 10.

Leaves: Make three templates, and cut each size twice in olive green crêpe. Glue the smallest pair round the stem, opposite one another, the tips half-way up the sepals. Glue the next pair 1 inch (25 mm) below, their tips falling *between* the leaves above. Glue the final pair 1 inch (25 mm) lower, their tips falling between the middle leaves.

Cup each leaf slightly (page 8) across the widest point (see illustration). Then gently stretch the blue crêpe across the base of the short petals, and stroke the long ones (page 8), to curl back as shown.

Japanese & St. Brigid Anemones

Just three of the long-stemmed hybrid anemones would make a striking display in a tall vase; the vibrantly coloured heads of the smaller Saint Brigid variety are at their best when tightly bunched.

Japanese Anemones

Materials: Very pale pink crêpe paper for petals ⎫ or one
Pinky-mauve (lilac) crêpe paper for petals ⎬ colour only
Deep yellow crêpe paper for stamens
Olive green crêpe paper for stem
Lime green soft-ply tissue (or substitute) for centre
Plastic-covered garden wire
Sewing thread or fine wire
Cotton wool
Solid stick adhesive (optional)
Fabric adhesive or rubber cement

WINDFLOWERS

Stem and centre: Cut a 12 inch (30 cm) length of garden wire, turn over ⅜ inch (10 mm) at one end, then wrap and glue cotton wool around it to form a round ball about ¾ inch (20 mm) in diameter (diagram 1).

Cut a 3 inch (8 cm) diameter circle of lime green tissue, place the centre over the top of the cotton wool ball, draw the edges down smoothly all round, and bind tightly underneath with thread or wire (diagram 2).

Cut a piece of deep yellow crêpe paper, with grain as arrowed (diagram 3). Make a folded fringe strip (page 9) as diagram 4, snipping the folded edge very finely to a depth of about ½ inch (12 mm).

Glue the yellow strip round the base of the centre, keeping the cut edges of the yellow and green level.

Petals: Trace the pattern and make a template (page 8). Cut eight *double*

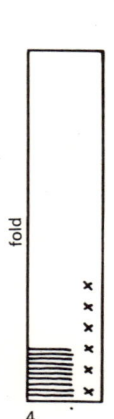

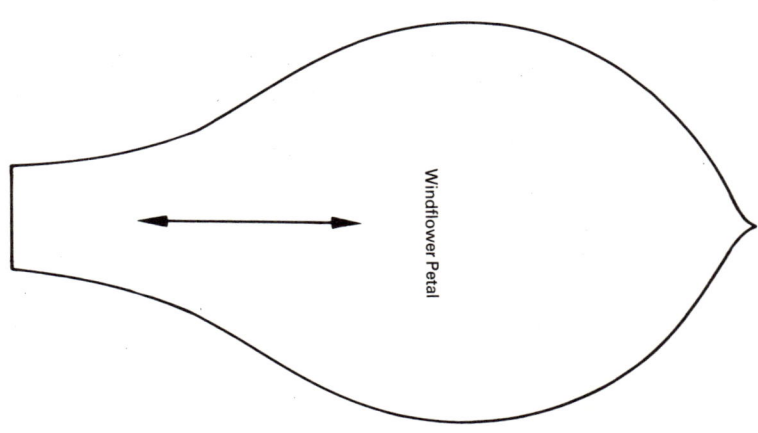

petals, pink on top and mauve underneath, or you can cut all in one colour (page 9). Make up as described on page 9.

Glue four petals (pink side up) evenly round the centre, lower edges of petal and fringe level. Then glue the remaining four petals behind the previous ones, the centre of each outer petal positioned directly between two inner ones. Glue a little cotton wool underneath the centre to round off the base. Then bind the base and stem as directed on page 10.

Cup the lower part of each outer petal (page 8), and stroke the tips (page 8) to curl back as illustrated. Draw these four petals down, then cup and curl the inner ones in the same way.

Bunch of Saint Brigid Anemones

Just like those clustered on a street-seller's barrow – in as dramatic a selection of characteristic shades as you can find.

Materials: Crêpe paper for petals (scarlet, crimson, violet, purple, deep blue, white)
Black crêpe paper for centre
Olive green crêpe paper for foliage and stem
Plastic-covered garden wire
Sewing thread or fine wire
Cotton wool
Olive green drawing ink or water-colour (optional)
Fabric adhesive or rubber cement

Stem and centre: Cut a 9 inch (23 cm) length of garden wire, turn over ⅜ inch (10 mm) at one end, then wrap and glue cotton wool around it to form a flattish ball just over an inch (25 mm) in diameter (diagram 1).

Cut a 3½ inch (9 cm) circle of black crêpe paper, place the centre over the top of the cotton wool, stretching it slightly, and draw the edges smoothly down all round: bind tightly underneath with thread or wire (diagram 2). The diameter should now be just *under* an inch (25 mm).

Cut a piece of black crêpe with grain as arrowed (diagram 3). Fold in half as indicated, then snip the cut edges to a depth of two-thirds to form a fine fringe (diagram 4).

Wrap and glue the folded edge of the black strip round the base of the centre. Stroke the fringe (page 8) to curl *inwards*, over the centre.
Petals: Cut a piece of coloured crêpe with grain as arrowed (diagram 5). Fold in half, as indicated: then fold concertina-wise, at 1½ inch (40 mm) intervals, and cut as shown by the broken line on diagram 6.

Open out folds B, and cup each of the six double petals (page 8) fully at X. Glue the folded edge of the first three round the base of the centre, level with the lower edge of the black strip – gathering with the fingertips to distribute the petals evenly: then fix the remainder in the same way.
Foliage: Cut a piece of olive green crêpe with grain as arrowed (diagram 7). ★Fold in half as indicated, and snip the cut edges closely with pinking shears three-quarters way down, as diagram 8. Open out gently, to separate the serrated fringe, then re-crease, and glue the folded edge round the base of the flowers. Stroke the fringe so that the ends curl *inwards*, round the petals.

Glue a little cotton wool underneath to round off the base. Then bind the base and stem as directed on page 10. Re-cup and shape the petals, if necessary.

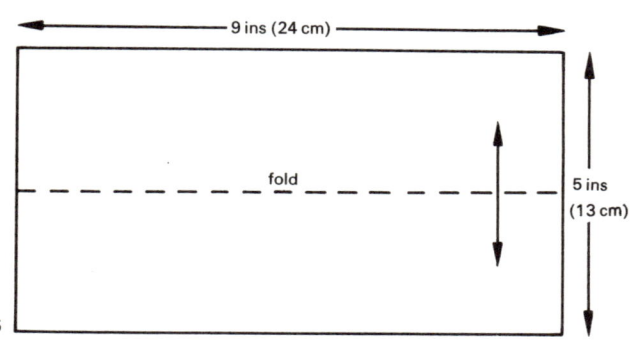

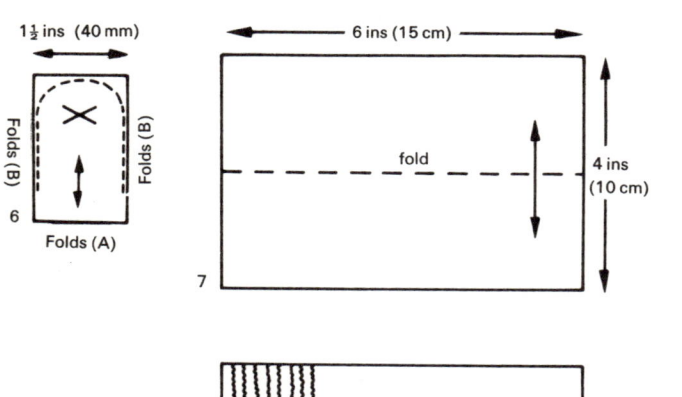

Bud – stem and centre: Cut a 9 inch (23 cm) length of garden wire, turn over $\frac{5}{8}$ inch (15 mm) at one end, and cover with a 1 inch (25 mm) square of black crêpe paper, glueing it round as diagram 9.

Petals: Cut a piece of coloured crêpe with grain as arrowed (diagram 10). Fold in half as indicated. Now cut another strip of crêpe – exactly the same as the first piece, but half the depth (2 inches–5 cm). Place this over the folded piece, and glue along the lower edge (x's on diagram 11) to form three thicknesses.

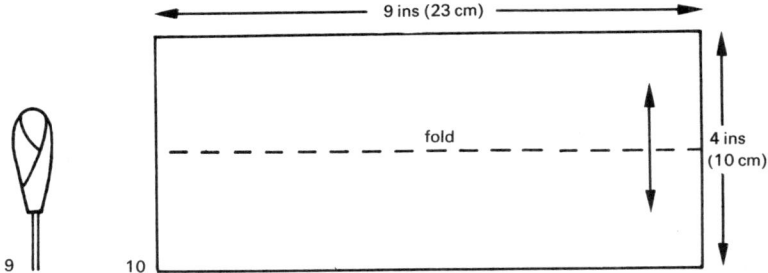

Fold the strip in half *along* the grain (fold B – diagram 12), and round off the corners as indicated by the broken line. Open out fold B. Now stretch the upper half of the strip as fully as possible, in one long, continuous 'cup' (page 8) (indicated by the wavy line on diagram 13) just above the centre.

Glue the folded edge round the centre, gathering with the fingertips into tightly clustered pleats, only lessening the gathers slightly for the final round.

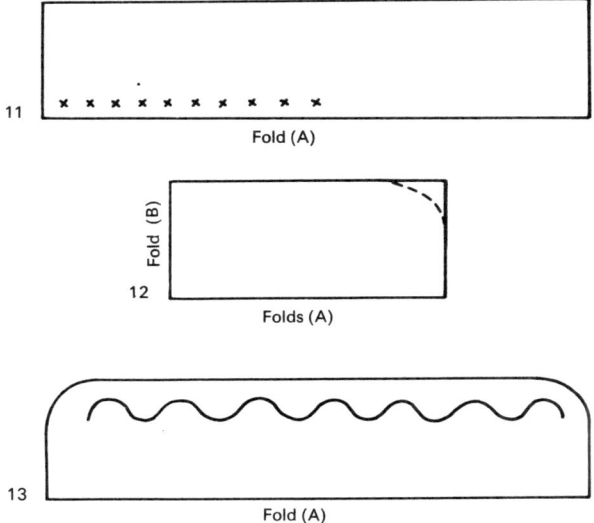

Foliage: Cut a piece of olive creen crêpe with grain as arrowed (diagram 14). Now follow the directions for the flower from ★ to complete the bud.

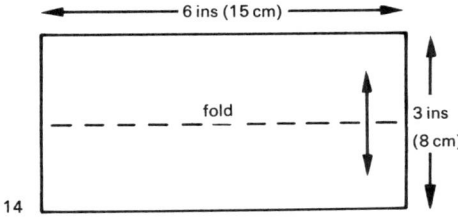

I tinted the white petals with slight touches of olive green here and there – moistening cotton wool with a little drawing ink, and gently wiping it over to leave just the merest smudge.

25

Marigolds, Marigolds

'Inch worm, inch worm, measuring the marigolds....' And measuring is all you have to do to make *these* – French or African, whichever you prefer!

Mixed French Marigolds

Directions are given for the flower with brown outer petals in the illustration on page 36: I made a second marigold in the same bright yellow and brown, except for the outer petals (strip D), which I cut in golden yellow. The third flower is like the second – but this time I used the golden yellow all through.

Materials: Bright yellow crêpe paper for petals
Brown crêpe paper for petals
Olive green crêpe paper for stem
Plastic-covered garden wire
Strong sewing thread
Cotton wool
Fabric adhesive or rubber cement

Stem and centre: Cut an 8 inch (20 cm) length of wire: then twist and glue a 1 inch (25 mm) square of yellow crêpe paper round one end – as diagram 1.

Cut two pieces of crêpe as diagram 2, one brown, one yellow (grain as arrows). Fold each in half as indicated. Place the yellow piece on top of the brown, folded edges level, and glue lower edges (x's on diagram 3). Now snip the folded edges closely to a depth of about $\frac{1}{2}$ inch (12 mm), as diagram 3.

With the yellow side inside, wrap and glue the lower edge tightly round the covered tip of the stem (diagram 4).
Petals: Cut four 9 inch (23 cm) wide strips of crêpe, to the measurements shown in diagram 5: cut A and B in yellow, and C and D in brown.

FRENCH MARIGOLD

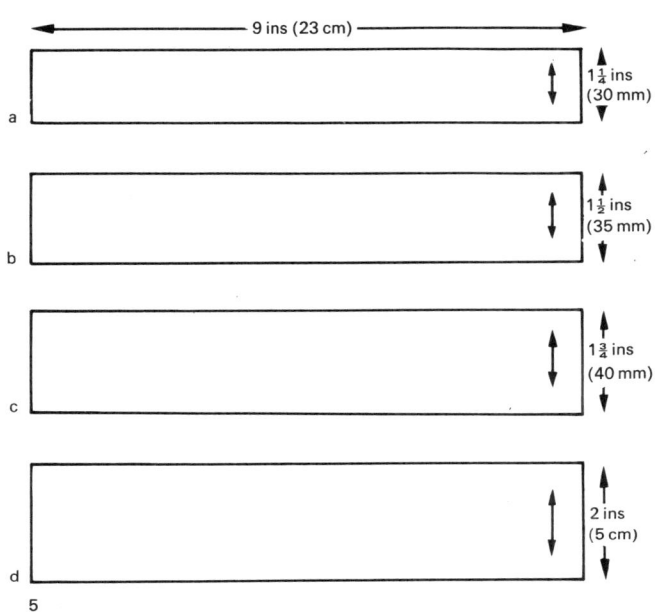

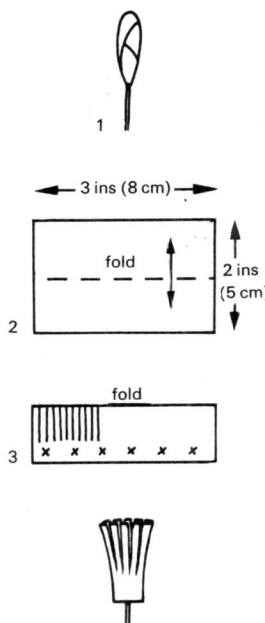

Prepare the petals as follows. Place strip A on a piece of smooth-surfaced waste paper: then, using a paint-brush, saturate the upper half of the crêpe with clear water, so that it forms a finely frilled edge (diagram 6). Set this piece aside to dry and do the next two strips *together*; place strip B on top of strip C, top and side edges level. Then brush the upper half with water as before, so the yellow and brown run into one another. When the yellow is tinged with brown, and the edges crinkled as before, gently pull the two strips apart and leave in a warm place on separate pieces of paper until dry.

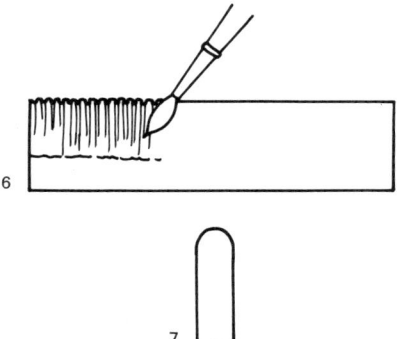

Fold strip D concertina-wise, along the grain, at $\frac{3}{4}$ inch (20 mm) intervals. Holding tightly together at the base, round off the top corners as diagram 7 – to a depth of $\frac{3}{4}$ inch (20 mm) at each side. Open out the strip, and snip down between any un-cut pairs of petals.

Now pin the four layers together, side and *lower* edges level: D underneath, then C, then B, with A on top. Thread a needle, and run a gathering thread about ⅜ inch (10 mm) above the lower edge (diagram 8). Draw up tightly and secure. Spread adhesive along the gathered edge of the top layer, and glue the petals round the centre, lower edges level, side edges meeting.

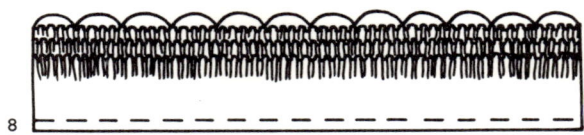

Glue a little cotton wool underneath, to round off the base. Then bind the base and stem as directed on page 10.

Gently pull apart the four layers of petals, separating the gathers: then stroke the outer brown petals (page 8), to curl them outwards.

African Marigolds

Directions are for the golden one: I made another in orange – and a third in bright yellow, with leaf green instead of olive for the centre.

Materials: Golden yellow crêpe paper for petals
Olive green crêpe paper for centre
Plastic-covered garden wire
Cotton wool
Thin split bamboo garden stakes (optional)
Adhesive tape (optional)
Fabric adhesive or rubber cement

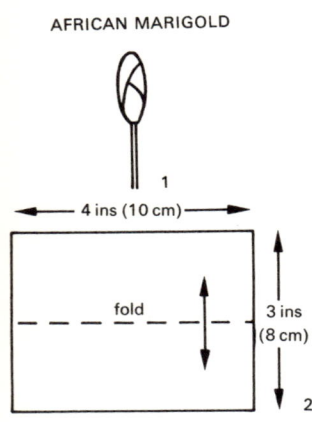

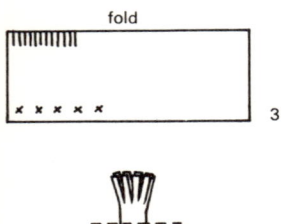

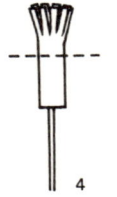

Stem and centre: Cut a 9 inch (23 cm) length of wire: then twist and glue a 1 inch (25 mm) square of yellow crêpe paper round one end, as diagram 1.

Cut two pieces of crêpe as diagram 2, one yellow, one olive (grain as arrows). Fold each strip in half, as indicated. Place the olive strip on top of the yellow, folded edges level, and glue lower edges (x's on diagram 3). Now snip the folded edges closely to a depth of about ¼ inch (5 mm) – diagram 3.

With the olive side inside, wrap and glue the lower edge tightly round the covered tip of the wire (diagram 4).

Petals: Cut five 12 inch (30 cm) wide strips of yellow crêpe, to the measurements shown in diagram 5.

Fold strip A in half, as indicated. Then snip the *cut* edges at ¼ inch (5 mm) intervals to a depth of half-way, as diagram 6. Stroke the snipped edges gently (page 8) to curl them slightly. Then spread adhesive close to the folded edge and, gathering tightly into pleats with the fingertips, and pinching together as you go, fix round the centre, the folded edge positioned as the broken line on diagram 4, so that the tops of the petals and centre are level. If you prefer, you can gather with a thread, as for the French marigold, drawing up the strip first and then glueing it into place.

Fold strip B, snip the cut edges half-way down, and curl, as strip A. Then glue round the centre in the same way, with the lower edge slightly below that of the previous piece.

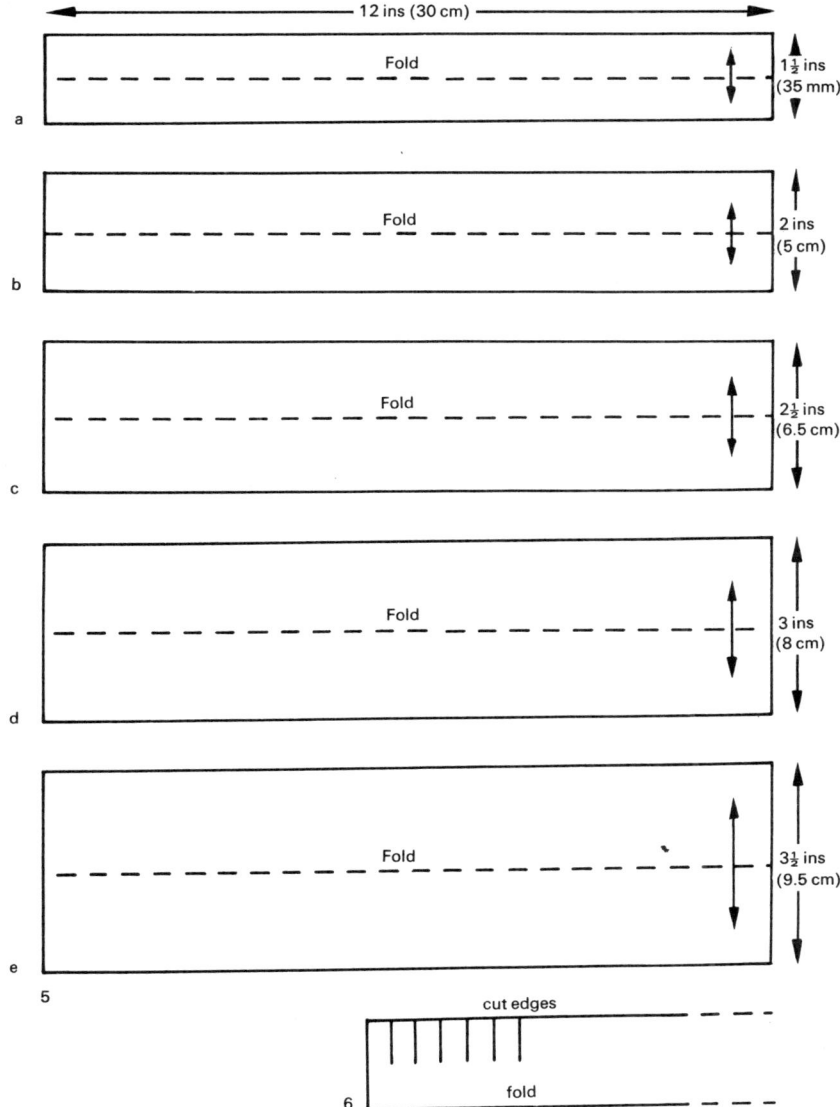

Repeat with strips C, D and E, always snipping to a depth of half-way, but making the cuts slightly wider apart as the strips grow deeper.

Glue a little cotton wool underneath to round off the base. (If your stem-wire bends under the weight of the flower-head, tape a thin garden stake alongside it for added support. See page 6.) Then bind the base and stem as directed on page 10.

Morning Glory & a Posy of Moss Roses

A romantic theme with a hint of nostalgia. The prettiest pink moss roses and buds in a tight bunch—and a long strand of morning glory.

Trailing Morning Glory

The flowers alone – with perhaps a single leaf for company – look charming in all kinds of situations: from a party decoration, set here and there on a buffet table, to more formal occasions, combined in a mixed floral display. But my own choice is a trailing creeper, which can be as long as you like.

Materials: Sky-blue crêpe paper for petals
White crêpe paper for centre
Light green crêpe paper for stems and leaf stalks
Olive green Duplex or single-weight crêpe paper for leaves
Fine soft wire
Very fine wire
Fabric adhesive or rubber cement

Stem and centre: Cut a 7 inch (18 cm) length of fine soft wire. Cut a length of white crêpe paper $\frac{1}{2}$ inch (10 mm) wide, with the grain running widthways, for binding (page 10).

Fold the end of the binding diagonally over the tip of the wire – as diagram 1: fold B over A, and bind down at least $1\frac{1}{2}$ inches (40 mm). Turn neatly and bind up to the top again, folding the binding over diagonally, level with the tip, as broken line on diagram 2. Now bind round, keeping the fold (diagram 3) level, to thicken the tip, before binding down to finish at the previous level.

Cut a piece of white crêpe with grain as arrowed (diagram 4). Make a folded fringe strip (page 9) as diagram 5, snipping the folded edge closely to a depth of half-way. Glue the strip fairly tightly round the bound wire, the top edge of the fringe about $\frac{1}{2}$ inch (15 mm) below the tip of the stem (diagram 6).
Petals: Trace the pattern, make a template (page 8), and cut five in sky-blue crêpe.

Place one petal on a flat surface. Take a second petal and spread a thin line of adhesive *behind* the left-hand edge, below x: then glue over the right-hand edge of the first petal, beginning at the bottom and positioning as indicated by the broken line – twisting the petal slightly on the way up, so that the overlap is the same width (about $\frac{1}{8}$ inch – 3 mm) all the way, tapering off at the widest point of the petal. Join a third petal to the second in the same way, followed by the remaining ones. Then glue the left-hand edge of the first petal over the last one, to form a circle.

Spread adhesive round the base of the centre (x-x on diagram 6), then gently lower the stem down through the cone of petals, until the lower edges of the petals and centre are level: pinch together.
Bind the stem with light green crêpe, as directed on page 10.

Sepals: Make a template for each. Cut two small sepals in light green crêpe, and two larger ones in olive green Duplex or single-weight crêpe. Stick the two light green sepals on opposite sides of the flower, corners overlapping. Cup the two dark ones (page 8) very slightly at X, and stick over the divisions between the lighter ones, as diagram 7.

Leaves: If you want individual flowers, with a single leaf attached, follow the appropriate directions below, preparing a 5–6 inch (12·5–15 cm) stalk, and using leaf patterns A or B, as preferred.

To make the full, eight-flower trailing stem with graduated leaves, cut the following lengths of fine soft wire:

6 pieces 6 inches (15 cm) long   6 pieces 4 inches (10 cm) long
11 pieces 5 inches (12·5 cm) long   2 pieces 3 inches (7·5 cm) long

And cut one piece of *very* fine wire 4 inches (10 cm) long.

Beginning with a neatly pointed tip (cut binding diagonally, as diagram 8), bind each 6 inch (15 cm) length of wire with a ½ inch (10 mm) wide strip of light green crêpe, to 1½ inches (40 mm) from the end. Place alongside the flower stem, cut ends of the wire level; bind together to the bottom.

MORNING GLORY

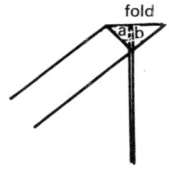

1

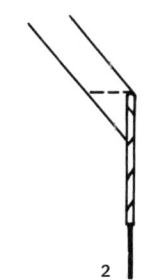

2

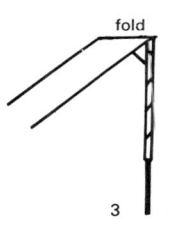

3

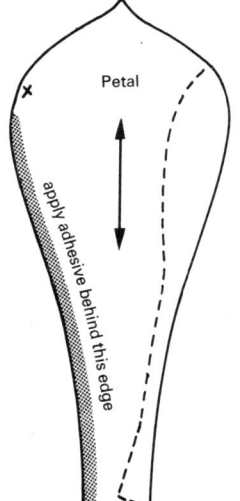

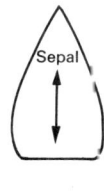

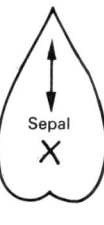

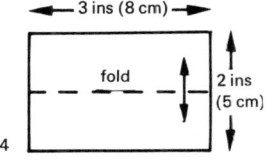

4

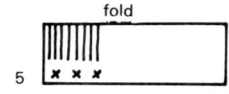

5

Bind two 5 inch (12·5 cm) wires, and join to the remaining flower stems.

Beginning with a pointed tip, bind all the remaining wires. Finish with the very fine wire – binding the lower 1½ inches (40 mm) to the base of a 4 inch (10 cm) stalk, as for the flowers.

Place the bottom inch of a 3 inch (7·5 cm) stalk alongside these two bound stalks, so that the cut end falls ½ inch (10 mm) below them – as diagram 9:

6

7

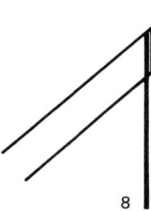

8

9

10

31

bind section between broken lines securely. Add the other 3 inch (7·5) stalk in the same way – at the other side of the stem – as diagram 10.

Place the lower 1½ inches (40 mm) of a 4 inch (10 cm) stalk alongside, so that the end comes 1 inch (25 mm) below the main stem: bind together. Then add three more 4 inch (10 cm) stalks in the same way.

Place the lower 2 inches (5 cm) of a bound flower stem and 5 inch (12·5 cm) stalk alongside, so that the end comes 1½ inches (40 mm) below the main stem – and bind together. Then bind in the lower 1½ inches (40 mm) of a single 5 inch (12·5 cm) stalk, allowing the end to fall 1 inch (25 mm) below the main stem. Add the other flower bound to a 5 inch (12·5 cm) stalk – exactly as described for the first one – followed by another single 5 inch (12·5 cm) stalk, bound on in the same way as the first.

Continue to add the remaining flowers (bound to 6 inch (15 cm) stalks), with a 5 inch (12·5 cm) single stalk between each.

Finally, turn the remaining 4 inch (10 cm) stalk so that the tip points down, place the end alongside the base of the main stem – overlapping about an inch (25 mm) – and bind neatly together.

Twist the upper half of the very fine stalk at the top round in a spiral, to form a curled tendril (see illustration).

Trace the four leaf patterns and make templates. Cut leaves in olive Duplex or single crêpe, as follows:

Leaf A: cut seven   Leaf C: cut four
Leaf B: cut eleven   Leaf D: cut three.

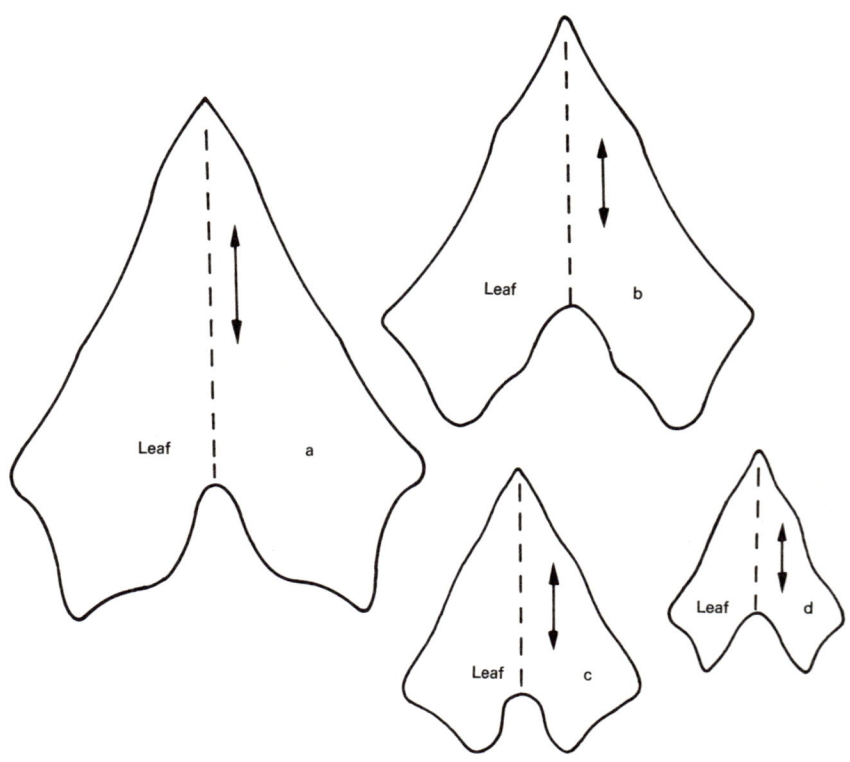

Position the leaves in the following order – glueing into place as described on page 11:

Tip of main stem (beside tendril), and the
 two 3 inch (7·5 cm) stalks below: leaves D
Next four 4 inch (10 cm) stalks: leaves C
Nex two 5 inch (12·5 cm) stalks: leaves B
Next two 5 inch (12·5 cm) *stalks combined with flowers*: leaves B
Seven single 5 inch (12·5 cm) *stalks between flowers*: leaves B
Remaining six 6 inch (15 cm) *stalks combined with flowers*: leaves A
Reversed 4 inch (10 cm) stalk at base of stem: leaf A
Bend the leaf stalks back at right angles to the stem, then curve them sharply round before shaping softly behind the leaves as shown.
Gently stretch the flower petals at the widest point, to curl back and open out as illustrated.

Posy of Old Pink Moss Roses

Dainty buds in various stages of opening – the perfect posy for a demure bridesmaid.

Materials: Medium pink crêpe paper for inner petals ⎫ or use only
Pale pink crêpe paper for outer petals ⎭ one shade
Olive green crêpe paper for foliage and stems
Deep olive/forest green Duplex crêpe paper for leaves (optional)
Soft-ply face tissues
Golden yellow raffia
Plastic-covered garden wire
Fine soft wire
Sewing thread (optional)
Solid stick adhesive (only if not using Duplex crêpe – and then optional)
Fabric adhesive or rubber cement

MOSS ROSE

Stem and centre: Cut a 6–7 inch (16–18 cm) length of garden wire, and two 1½ inch (40 mm) lengths of raffia. Turn over ⅜ inch (10 mm) at one end of the wire (diagram 1), and hook over the centre of the raffia (diagram 2). Bend the hook back and bind the raffia tightly with thread or wire, then trim the cut ends level (diagram 3). Finally, bind round the looped wire and raffia with a strip of pink crêpe, as diagram 4.

Petals: Cut two pieces of mid pink crêpe, and one piece of pale pink with grain as arrowed (diagram 5). Fold each strip in half across the grain, as indicated: then concertina-wise at 1 inch (25 mm) intervals along the grain; and cut as indicated by the broken line on diagram 6. Open out folds B and then cut along fold A, making each double strip into two single ones. Turn one strip over, and glue each pair of strips lightly together again along the lower edge – but positioned so that each top petal falls directly over the division between two underneath (diagram 7).

Cup each petal (page 8) low down at large X – diagram 8. Now curl back the top edges (page 8) of the pale pink petals *only*, as indicated by the broken lines on diagram 8.

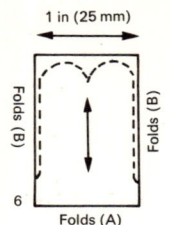
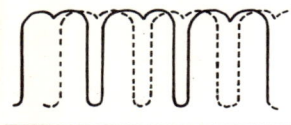
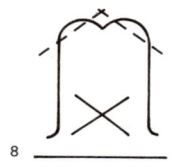

Wrap first one, and then the second, mid pink strip round the raffia centre, glueing the lower edge over the paper foundation, and keeping absolutely level. Wrap the first few petals round fairly tightly, then gradually roll the strip round more loosely, gathering the lower edge in neatly with the fingertips. Finally, add the pale pink strip, even more loosely, pinching in at the base as before. Use strips of face tissue as described on page 10, to round off the base of the flower and pad the stem.

Sepals: Trace the pattern, make a template (page 8), and cut once in olive green. Cup each sepal fully at X, then spread adhesive below the broken line and glue evenly round the flower.

Bind the base and stem as directed on page 10.

Tighter buds: Follow the directions above, but omit the paler pink petals; this will make a fairly full bud. For a closer bud, use just one double strip of mid pink petals or, for a tight bud, use only half a double strip.

Pad base and bind stem with face tissue, as directed.

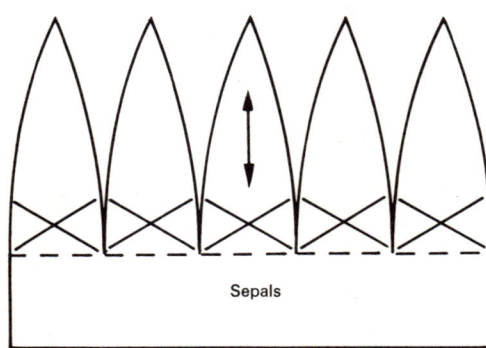
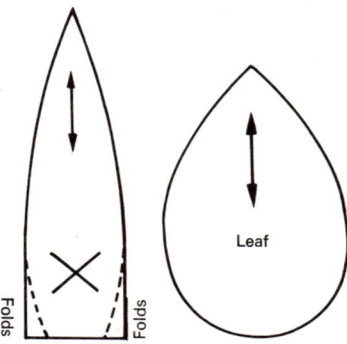

Bud sepals: For the largest bud, follow the main directions. But for a medium or tiny bud, take a set of joined sepals (as pattern), fold concertina-wise as diagram 9 and trim each side as indicated by the broken line. Cup each individual sepal slightly at X, then glue evenly round the bud and bind.

Leaves: I left my largest roses without leaves, but added a spray to each bud.

Cut three pieces of fine soft wire – one $5\frac{1}{2}$ inches (14 cm) long, and two $3\frac{1}{2}$ inches (9 cm) long. Beginning with a neatly pointed tip (page 10), bind the longer piece as directed on page 10, finishing 1 inch (25 mm) from the end.

Again making a pointed tip, bind a shorter piece for $1\frac{1}{2}$ inches (40 mm) and place alongside the first stalk, the tip 1 inch (25 mm) below the tip of the long one. Continue binding the two together to the bottom. Bind the second short wire in the same way, then align it on the other side of the long stalk, level with the first short one, and bind all three together for 1 inch (25 mm).

Align the remainder of the leaf stalks alongside the main stem, so that the tip of the longest stalk is about $\frac{3}{4}$–1 inch (20–25 mm) above the flower – and bind all together to the bottom of the stem.

Trace the leaf pattern and make a template. Cut three leaves with jagged edges (page 11) in Duplex crêpe; or bond two pieces of single-weight crêpe together (page 9); or just use single thickness. Glue one leaf over each stalk (page 11), and curve the wires back so that the leaves curl over slightly, as illustrated.

Japanese and St Brigid Anemones (pages 22 and 23)

Love-in-a-mist & Carnations

Love-in-a-mist can be pink or white, as well as the more usual pale blue. I have kept to the traditional carnation colours, because I prefer them, but you can be as imaginative as you like, and create a selection of blooms in the unlikeliest hues!

Feathery Love-in-a-Mist

The flower has a rather unusual centre, composed of bracts – which makes it particularly effective as a simple arrangement in a plain vase. I bonded two shades of green together to make it more distinctive: but if you haven't the deeper shade, just use light green alone, either bonded or single-weight.

Materials:
 Light blue crêpe paper for petals
 Light green crêpe paper for centre, bracts and foliage
 Grass green crêpe paper for bracts (optional)
 White crêpe paper for stamens
 Soft-ply face tissues
 Plastic-covered garden wire
 Sewing thread or fine wire
 Cotton wool
 Solid stick adhesive (optional)
 Fabric adhesive or rubber cement

Stem and centre: Cut a 10 inch (25 cm) length of garden wire, turn over ¼ inch (5 mm) at one end, then wrap and stick cotton wool around it to form a round ball about ⅝ inch (15 mm) in diameter.

Cut a 2½ inch (6 cm) diameter circle of light green crêpe paper, place the centre over the top of the cotton wool ball, draw the edges down smoothly all round, and bind tightly with thread or wire (diagram 1).

Bracts: Cut one piece each light green and grass green crêpe with grain as arrowed (diagram 2). Bond together (page 9). Then fold concertina-wise, along the grain (as broken lines), into five. Trace the bract pattern, make a template (page 8) and cut five bracts in the two-tone crêpe.

Light green side uppermost, stretch each bract across the widest part (arrowed in diagram 3). Fold the sides up (as broken lines), so that the edges overlap in the centre (diagram 4). Spread adhesive over the little light green section at the base, marked x: then glue x to the flower centre, lower edge of bract level with thread or wire (diagram 5). Glue the remaining four bracts equally round the centre, adjusting the spacing, if necessary. Now place a dab of adhesive inside each bract at o (diagram 4), and draw the bracts neatly together at the top.

Stamens: Cut a piece of white crêpe with grain as arrowed (diagram 6). Make a folded fringe strip (page 9) as diagram 7, snipping the folded edge very closely to half-way.

Marigolds, French and African (pages 26 and 28)

LOVE-IN-A-MIST

1

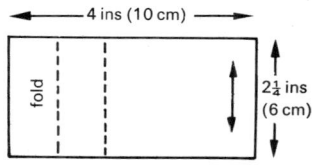

2

Glue the white strip round the base of the centre, with the lowest point of the cuts level with the thread or wire (diagram 8).

Stroke each bract (page 8) so that it curls right round and under, finishing off with the fingertips, if necessary (diagram 9).

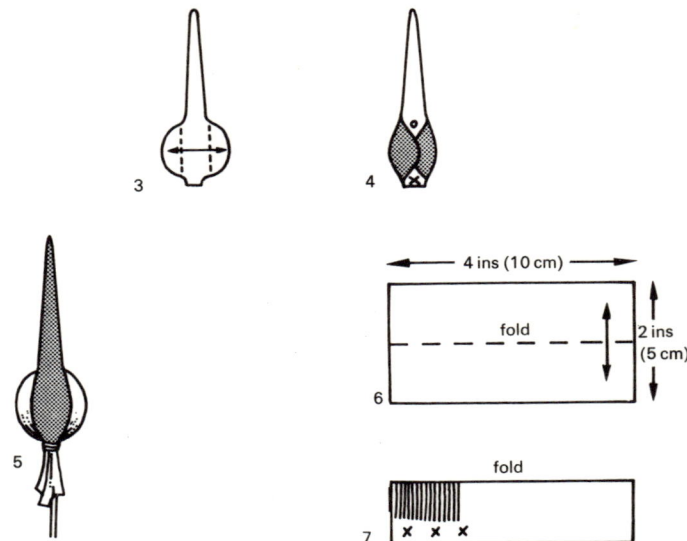

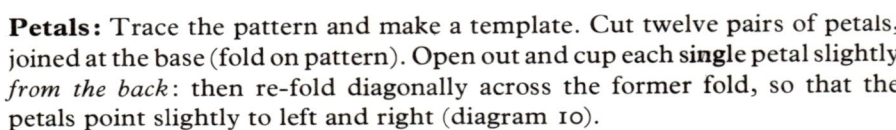

Petals: Trace the pattern and make a template. Cut twelve pairs of petals, joined at the base (fold on pattern). Open out and cup each **single** petal slightly *from the back*: then re-fold diagonally across the former fold, so that the petals point slightly to left and right (diagram 10).

Glue three pairs of petals equally round the centre. Then glue three more pairs, falling between the first ones. Add three more pairs behind the first round and the final three pairs behind the second round.

Use a strip of face tissue as described on page 10, to pad under the centre and form a rounded base.

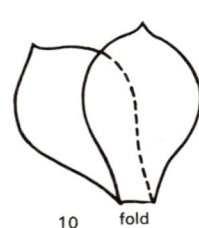
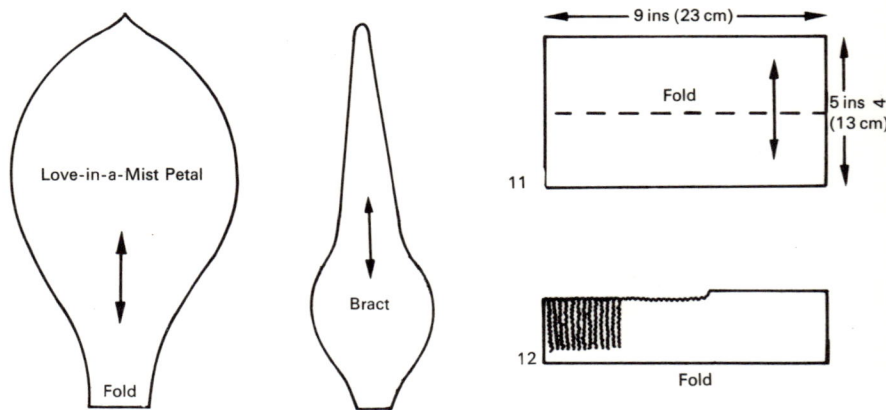

Foliage: Cut a piece of light green crêpe with grain as arrowed (diagram 11). Fold in half, as indicated. Using pinking shears, trim away the straight top edges (diagram 12). Then cut the pinked edge closely, to within ½ inch (10 mm) of the lower, folded edge (diagram 12). Glue round the flower, close under the petals. Then bind the base and stem as directed on page 10.

Prize Carnations

These just *have* to win first prize as the biggest, boldest and most beautiful — and would make a striking party or reception decoration.

Materials: *Crêpe paper for petals (pink, red, white, or your choice)*
Silvery-green (or light green) crêpe paper for leaves and stems
Soft-ply face tissues
Plastic-covered garden wire
Fine soft wire
Fabric adhesive or rubber cement

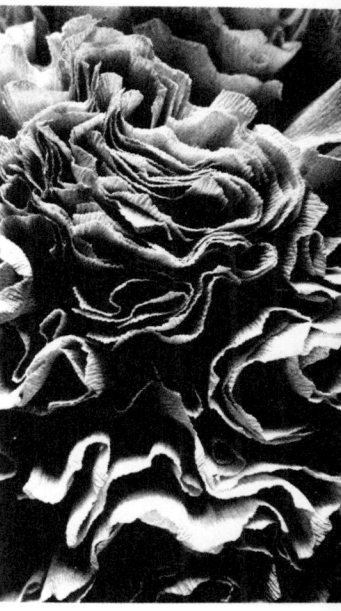

Centre: Cut a piece of crêpe paper with grain as arrowed (diagram 1). Fold in half, as indicated, right side *inside*. Trim the top (cut) edge with pinking shears, as diagram 2. Cut the double paper to about ¾ inch (20 mm) from the folded edge, snipping every ½ inch (15 mm) or so (let the pinked edge determine the exact measurement; I cut between every third notch).

Frill (page 8) each double petal at X. Then open out and refold right side

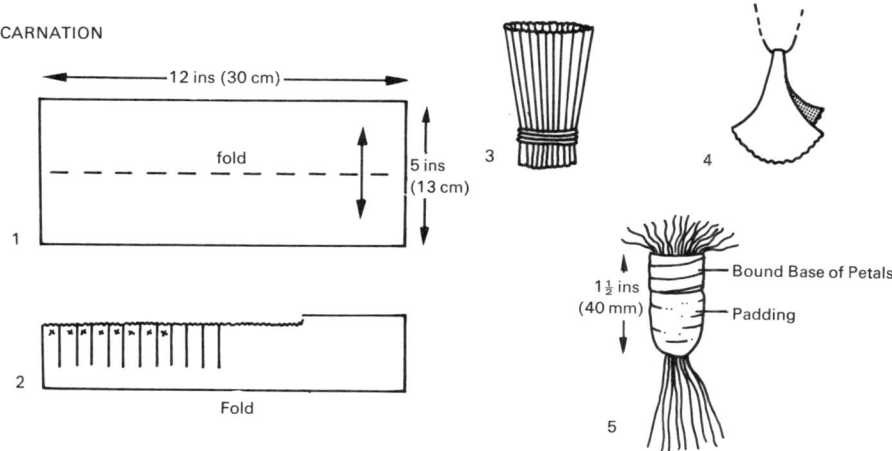
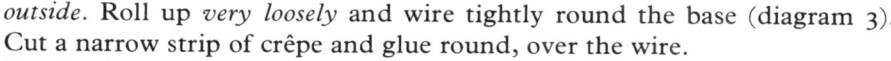

outside. Roll up *very loosely* and wire tightly round the base (diagram 3). Cut a narrow strip of crêpe and glue round, over the wire.

Petals: Trace the pattern and make a template (page 8). Cut thirty-six pairs of petals, joined at the base (fold on pattern): cut the side edges with scissors and around the top with pinking shears. Open out and frill each petal round the top edge. Then fold up again.

Cut a 24 inch (60 cm) length of fine, soft wire, and bend it in half. One-by-one, link nine petals over the wire, the fold held in the loop (diagram 4) — pushing the bases tightly together, and then twisting the wire below to hold them securely. Glue the bunch of petals beside the centre, top edges of both sets of petals level.

Make three more sets of petals. Glue the second bunch to the other side of the centre, and the remaining two sets between. Bind round the base, as before.

Base of flower: Use strips of face tissue padding as described on page 10, to build up the elongated, rounded base, continuing until the bottom of the petals plus the padding measures about 1½ inches (40 mm) — as diagram 5. Bind with petal-coloured crêpe (page 10).

Sepals: Make a template, and cut in silvery-green crêpe. Wrap round the base of the flower, overlapping as broken line, and glue the side overlap.

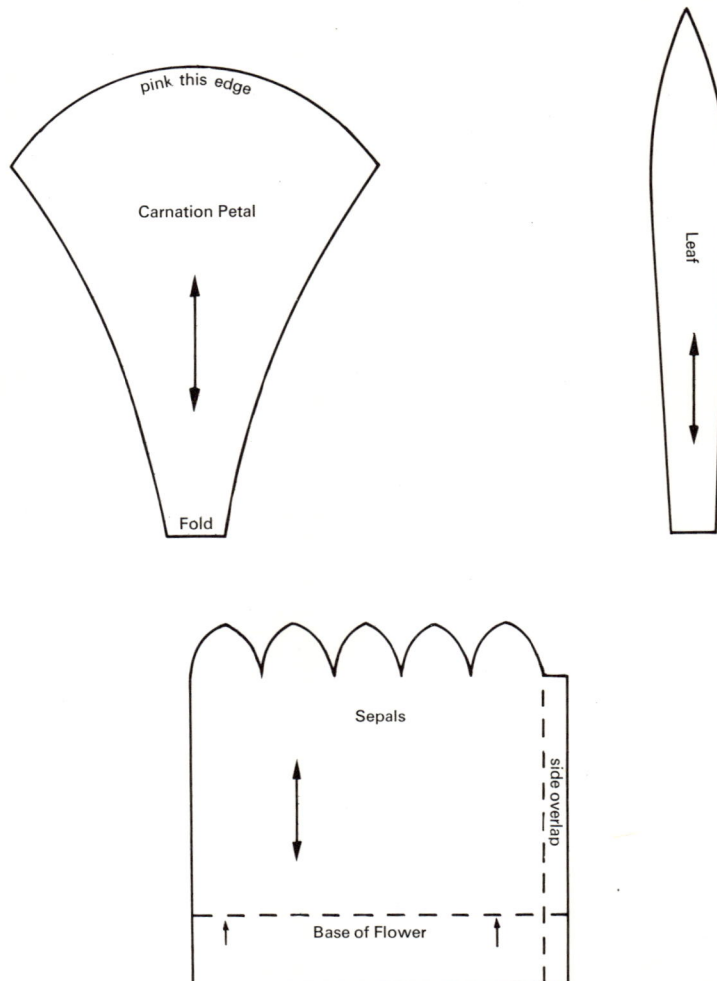

Stem: Cut an 11 inch (28 cm) length of garden wire and push one end up into the base of the flower, between the thin wires. Then bind all the wires together with strips of face tissue, to form a firm, padded stem (see page 10). Finally, bind the stem with silvery-green crêpe, as directed on page 10.

Leaves: Make a template and cut four. Glue round the stem in pairs, and stroke the upper half (page 8) to curl the tips over.

Fluff out the petals.

Asters & Tiger Lilies

Two jewel-coloured favourites from a summer garden, demonstrating a complete contrast of method: curling petals clustered round a close centre for the asters – and long stamens surrounded by dramatic, wired petals for the lily.

China Asters

These tightly massed layers of curled petals nestling in frothy greenery make a splendid subject for paper. Colours can range from pure white through creamy yellow, every shade of pink and mauve, to deepest purple.

Materials: *Crêpe paper for petals (pale yellow, pink, crimson violet, purple, etcetera)*
Primrose yellow crêpe paper for centre
White crêpe paper for centre
Light green crêpe paper for centre and foliage
Olive green crêpe paper for foliage
Soft-ply face tissues
Plastic-covered garden wire
Sewing thread or fine wire
Thin split bamboo garden stakes
Cotton wool
Adhesive tape
Fabric adhesive or rubber cement

Stem and centre: Cut a 13 inch (33 cm) length of garden wire, turn over

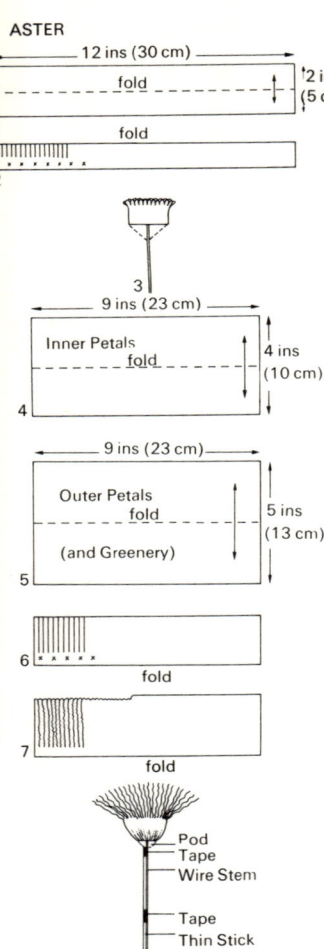

¼ inch (5 mm) at one end, then wrap and glue cotton wool around it to form a ball about the size of a small pea.

Cut a 2 inch (5 cm) diameter circle of light green crêpe paper, place the centre over the top of the cotton wool ball and draw the edges down smoothly all round. Bind tightly underneath with thread or wire.

Cut one piece of crêpe paper each in light green, primrose yellow and white with grain as arrowed (diagram 1). Make each into a folded fringe strip (page 9) as diagram 2, snipping the folded edge closely to a depth of about ⅜ inch (10 mm).

Keeping the snipped top edge exactly level with the covered centre, glue the green strip round the base of the centre, then the yellow strip, and then the white, all with lower edges absolutely level (diagram 3).

Cut a face tissue into four strips and use to form a padded base, as indicated by the broken line in diagram 3, spreading plenty of adhesive over the underside of the centre.

Petals: For the inner petals, cut two strips of coloured crêpe with grain as arrowed (diagram 4). For the outer petals, cut three strips as diagram 5. Fold each strip in half, as indicated, and then cut the double edge at approximately ⅛ inch (3 mm) intervals, to within ½ inch (10 mm) of the lower, folded edge (diagram 6).

Beginning with the two inner strips, glue each loosely round the centre, positioning the lower edge of the strips ½ inch (10 mm) below the centre, overlapping the padded base. Keep the lower edges of the strips level, but after adding each strip, pinch the folded edges neatly together – gradually forming a curved hollow.

Foliage: Cut one strip each in light and olive green, as the outer petals, diagram 5. Fold as for the petals, and cut in the same way – but use pinking shears, and first trim away the straight top edges to make a pinked line (diagram 7). Glue the light green strip round the petals – followed by the olive strip.

Tape a thin garden stake 12 inches (30 cm) long alongside the wire stem, with the top ¼–½ inch (5–10 mm) below the base of the padded centre (diagram 8). Pad the hollow and round off the base to meet the stick, as indicated by the broken line. Then bind the base and stem as directed on page 10.

Stroke the *petals only* (page 8), to curl them round as illustrated.

Tiger Lilies

Use this pattern for any kind of lily, curling the petals back rather less for trumpet or pure white Madonna lilies, but following the shape of the tiger lily for the beautiful pale pink variety which is spotted with deep crimson. White, yellow and pink lilies generally have golden yellow or dark orange stamens.

Materials: Orange crêpe paper for petals
Brown crêpe paper for stamens
Light green crêpe paper for stamens
Olive green crêpe paper for leaves and stem
Plastic-covered garden wire
Pipe cleaners
Rose wires (or very fine wire)
Brown felt pen or painting stick or drawing ink
Adhesive tape
Solid stick adhesive
Fabric adhesive or rubber cement

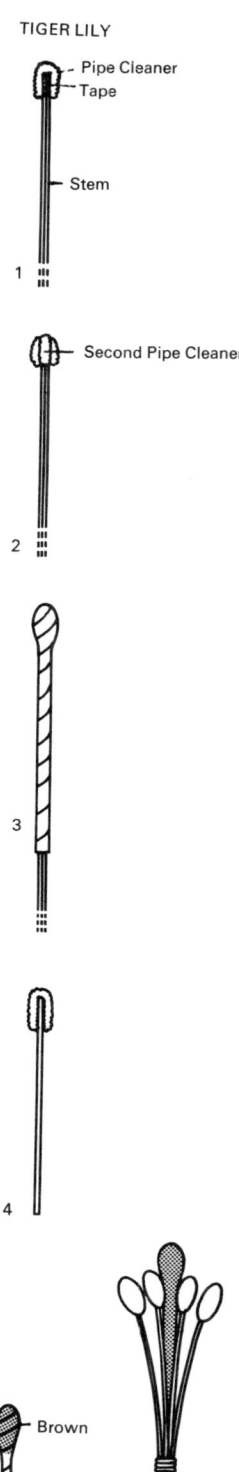

TIGER LILY

Stem and centre: Cut four 18 inch (45 cm) lengths of garden wire, and tape together at each end and in the middle. Cut a 1 inch (25 mm) length of pipe cleaner, bend it in half, and glue it over one end of the stem (diagram 1). Glue a ½ inch (12 mm) length of pipe cleaner at each side, between the first piece (diagram 2).

Beginning 4½ inches (11 cm) below the tip, bind with a ¼ inch (5 mm) wide strip of brown crêpe paper as directed on page 10 – up to and over the pipe cleaners at the top, and returning down over the previous binding to end neatly at the point where it began (diagram 3). Bind the remainder of the stem with ⅜ inch (10 mm) wide olive crêpe.

Stamens: Cut six 4 inch (10 cm) lengths of garden wire, and six 2 inch (5 cm) lengths of pipe cleaner. Bend each piece of pipe cleaner in half and glue one over one end of each piece of wire (diagram 4). Beginning and ending at the bottom, as previously, bind the entire stamen with a ¼ inch (5 mm) wide strip of light green crêpe. Then bind the top inch (25 mm), over the pipe cleaner, with brown crêpe (diagram 5).

Group the stamens round the top of the stem, so that the tips of the stamens are all level – ½ inch (12 mm) below the tip of the brown centre (diagram 6). Wire securely round the base, then bind over the wire with crêpe.

Petals: Trace the two patterns and make templates (page 8). Cut three *double* petals (page 9) each in orange crêpe. Make up each petal as described on page 9, but draw a line of dry adhesive down the centre and lay a fine rose wire along it before pressing the upper layer down. Trim the edges neatly. Mark irregular dark brown spots over each petal – denser on the lower half and decreasing towards the tip.

Glue the three inner petals round the centre, keeping the bases of the petals and stamens level. Then glue the three outer petals round to fall exactly between the inner ones. Bind the base neatly with crêpe.

Leaves: Make a template and cut two or three leaves in olive green crêpe. Then bind the stem again, and glue the leaves round at intervals.

Stroke the petals (page 8) to curl them over, finishing off round the

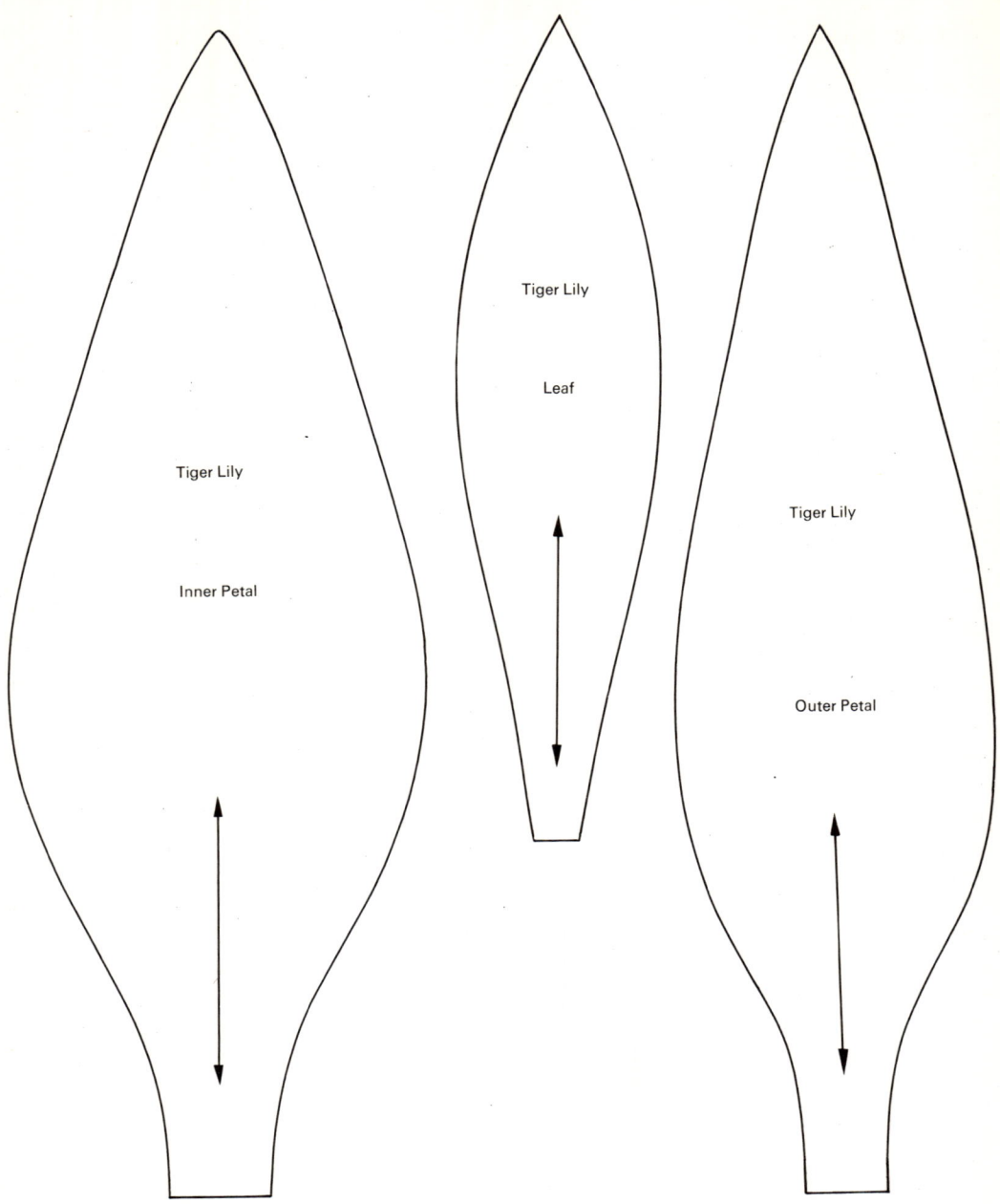

fingertips. Then gently stretch across the broadest part, cupping it slightly from underneath (page 8), where it curves over. Arrange the stamens neatly – spreading outwards slightly, as shown.

Make a second flower, with a 15 inch (38 cm) stem, and bind the two together for 4–6 inches (10–15 cm) at the base.

Morning Glory and Moss Roses (pages 30 and 33)
Love-in-a-Mist and Carnations (pages 37 and 39)

Canterbury Bells & Ranunculus

Once wild-flowers of the countryside, now tamed to grow happily captive in the garden. Here are Canterbury bells, in delicate shades of deep pink, pinky-mauve and blue. The buttercup is a humble member of the Ranunculus family; the cultivated double variety portrayed here is a great deal more dramatic! Pure white petals surrounding the strongly contrasted dark centre look particularly fresh and fragile: while a mixed bunch composed from the whole spectrum of sunshine colours makes a stunningly pretty posy.

Canterbury Bells

Materials: Crêpe paper for petals (blue, white, pink or mauve)
White crêpe paper for centres
Olive green crêpe paper for leaves and stem
Soft-ply face tissues
Light green raffia
Plastic-covered garden wire
Fine soft wire
Sewing thread (optional)
Fabric adhesive or rubber cement

Stalk and centre: For each flower, cut three pieces of light green raffia, 4 inches (10 cm) long; and one 3 inch (7·5 cm) length of fine soft wire (diagram 1). Place these together, the top of the wire 1 inch (25 mm) below the raffia strands.

Cut a narrow strip of white crêpe paper about ¼ inch (5 mm) wide by 3–4 inches (8–10 cm) long, with the grain running widthways. Begin binding the raffia and wire tightly together 1½ inches (40 mm) from the top (page 10).

CANTERBURY BELL

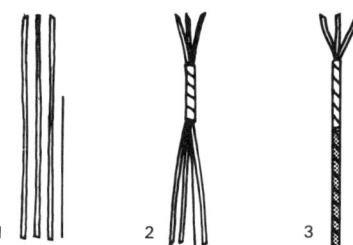

Bind up to 1 inch (25 mm) from the top of the raffia (level with the top of the wire), then turn and bind back about 1½ inches (40 mm): glue the end (diagram 2). Cut a narrow strip of olive green crêpe paper exactly as the white one, and use to bind the remainder of the stalk, beginning ¾ inch (20 mm) below the top of the white binding (diagram 3).

Asters and Tiger Lilies (pages 41 and 43)
Canterbury Bells and Ranunculus (pages 49 and 51)

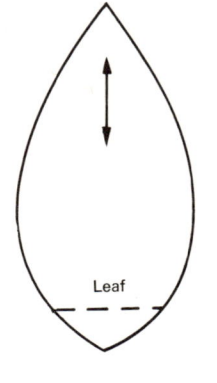
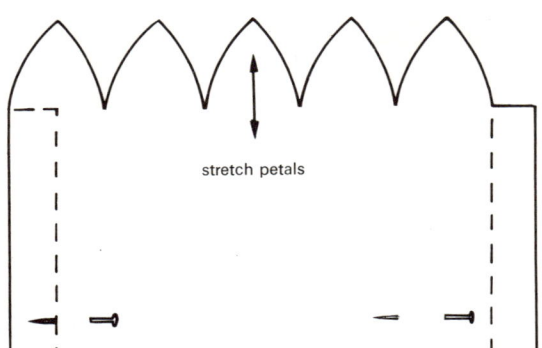
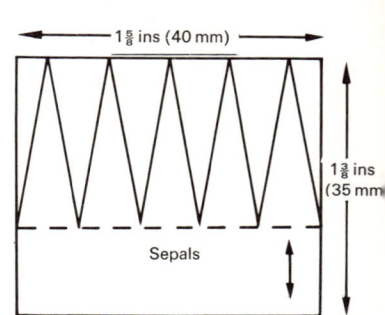

stretch petals

Leaf

Sepals

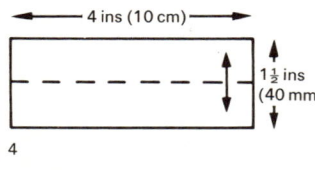
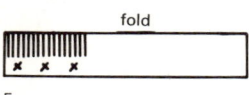
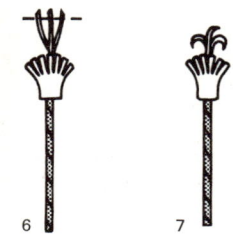
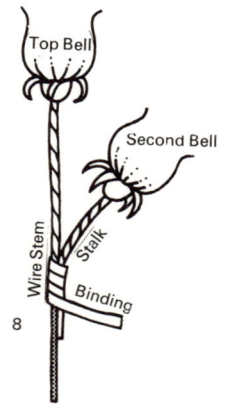

Cut a piece of white crêpe with grain as arrowed (diagram 4). Make a folded fringe strip (page 9) as diagram 5, snipping the folded edge closely to a depth of half-way. Glue the strip round the stalk, the fringed top edge level with the top of the white binding (diagram 6).

Trim the tips of the raffia so that it stands ¾ inch (20 mm) above the white fringe (broken line on diagram 6). Stroke each strand firmly several times (page 8), until it curls round and back: then trim each cut end to a point (diagram 7).

Petals: Trace the pattern and cut out to make a template. You will need five sets for each complete 'spike': to cut them all together, fix the tracing paper template to the folded layers of crêpe with tiny pins as indicated on the pattern (grain as arrows). This holds the template very flat to cut round the petals and in this position, the pin-marks won't show.

Carefully stretch the petals in a continuous 'cup' (page 8), as indicated, mid-way between the tips and base. Then curve round and glue the flap to the *outside*, overlapping the other side edge as indicated. Now place your left thumb up inside the flower, and gently stroke the petals (page 8) so that the tips curl back as illustrated.

Drop the stalk down through the middle of the bell and gather the base of the petals evenly round, lower edges of petals and centre level: bind tightly with thread or wire. Gently push out the gathers at the base to emphasise the bell-shape.

Sepals: Cut a piece of olive green crêpe as indicated (either freehand, or first tracing the pattern to make a template). Spread adhesive below the horizontal broken line, and gather evenly round the flower, the lower edge slightly overlapping the base of the petals: smooth this excess neatly round underneath. Stroke the sepals to curl back.

Make up five flowers in this way – four exactly as directed – but the fifth ignoring the direction to bind the stalk with green crêpe.

Stem: To make up the complete 'spike' cut a 12 inch (30 cm) length of garden wire, and push one end up between the strands of raffia forming the un-bound stalk of the final flower – until it reaches the base of the sepals. Then bind the raffia stalk as previously, including the garden wire. At the end of the raffia, place the *lower half* of another flower stalk alongside the wire, and continue binding the two together (diagram 8). At the bottom of this stalk, bind another flower to the wire. Add the remaining two flowers in the same way as before.

When you reach the bottom of the last stalk, bind the rest of the wire with a strip of face tissue, to pad it – as described on page 10. Then bind the padded stem with green crêpe – either the same narrow width as before, or the usual ½ inch (10 mm) wide binding.

Leaves: Trace the pattern and make a template. Cut five leaves. Slightly cup the centre of each, then spread adhesive below the broken line and wrap smoothly round the stem: position one leaf half-way down the stalk of the top flower – and the others underneath the four flowers, where the individual stalk joins the main stem (see picture).

Curve the stem, and the individual stalks, gently round, pulling the leaves back a little, as shown.

Ranunculus from the Rockery

The formation of the thick circle of extravagantly-coloured petals, clustered round a partially hidden pool of dark brown fringed with black, suggests a small, many-petalled poppy crossed with an anemone. Their almost 'unreal' quality makes ranunculus all the easier to reproduce in paper. This is one of the simplest and quickest designs in the book and ideal for mass-production if you want a quantity for decoration.

Materials: *Crêpe paper for petals (scarlet, pink, orange, yellow, white)*
  Black crêpe paper for centre
  Olive green crêpe paper for sepals and stem
  Dark brown soft-ply paper napkin or tissue (or crêpe) for centre
  Soft-ply face tissues
  Plastic-covered garden wire
  Sewing thread or fine wire
  Cotton wool
  Felt pens or drawing inks (optional)
  Fabric adhesive or rubber cement

RANUNCULUS

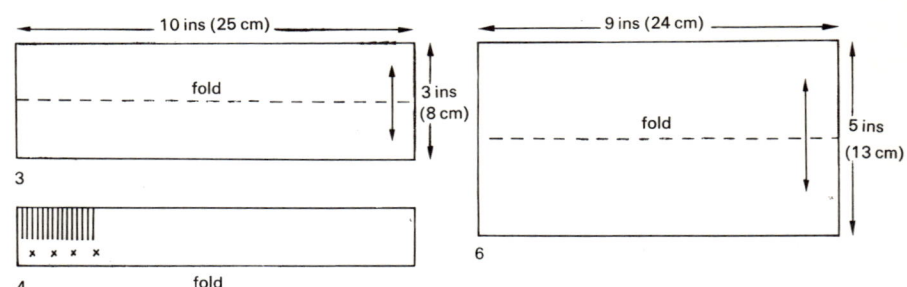

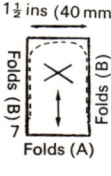

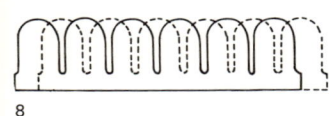

Stem and centre: Cut a 9 inch (23 cm) length of garden wire, turn over ⅜ inch (10 mm) at one end, then wrap and glue cotton wool around it to form a flattish ball about 1⅛ inches (30 mm) in diameter (diagram 1).

Cut a 3½ inch (9 cm) circle of dark brown paper napkin: place the centre over the top of the cotton wool, draw the edges smoothly down all round, and bind tightly underneath with thread or wire (diagram 2). The diameter of your centre should now be about an inch (25 mm).

Cut a piece of black crepe paper – grain as arrows, diagram 3. Fold in half as indicated, then snip the cut edges two-thirds of the way down, to form a fine fringe (diagram 4). Glue the lower edge (x's on diagram 4) loosely round the centre, the folded edge level with the cut edge of the brown paper. Pinch tightly together underneath while still wet. Stroke the fringe (page 8) to curl *inwards*, over the centre (diagram 5).

Petals: Cut three pieces of coloured crêpe with grain as arrowed (diagram 6). Fold each piece in half, as indicated; then fold concertina-wise, at 1½ inch (40 mm) intervals and cut as shown by the broken line on diagram 7.

Open out folds B and then cut along fold A – making each double strip into two single ones. Glue each pair lightly together again along the lower edge, but positioned so that each top petal falls directly over the division between two underneath (diagram 8). Now cup each petal fully (page 8) at X on diagram 7.

Ranunculus petals are sometimes marked with another colour: I streaked one yellow flower with bright crimson – flicking a quick line up the centre of each cupped petal with a felt pen.

Glue the lower edge of one double strip of petals loosely round the centre (lower edges level), gathering in with the fingertips, and pinching together neatly underneath. Add the second and third strips in the same way, but gather rather more than the first one, so that the petals stand away from the centre more loosely.

Sepals: Cut a piece of olive green crêpe as indicated (either freehand, or first tracing the pattern to make a template). Spread adhesive below the horizontal broken line, and wrap evenly round the base of the flower, lower edges level.

Use a strip of face tissue padding underneath the centre to form a rounded base, as described on page 10.

Bind the base and stem as directed on page 10. Then stroke the sepals so that they curl back and down, as illustrated.

Petunias & Pin Cushions

Two familiar garden flowers – but completely different. Contrast the delicate clear blue frilly petals of the scabious, with the vibrant pinks, mauves and purples of the petunias.

Pink and Purple Petunias

This design relies a great deal on the stretching qualities of the paper: so make sure you use good quality crêpe. And for a specially effective flower, combine paler and deeper shades of the same colour for the petals.

Materials: *Crêpe paper for petals (pink, red, mauve, purple, white)*
Paler shades of above crêpes for outside (optional)
Light green crêpe paper for sepals and stem
White crêpe paper for centre
Plastic-covered garden wire
Sewing thread or fine wire
Cotton wool
Solid stick adhesive
Fabric adhesive or rubber cement

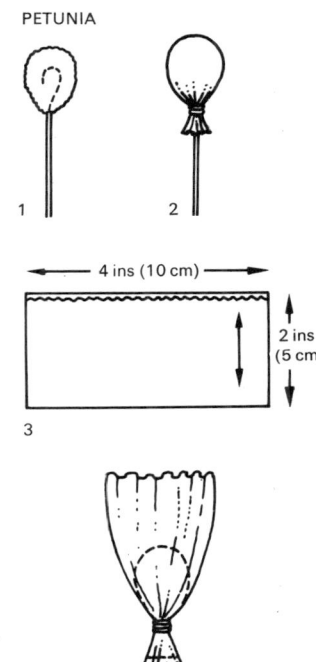

PETUNIA

Stem and centre: Cut a 10 inch (25 cm) length of garden wire, turn over ¼ inch (5 mm) at one end, then wrap and glue cotton wool around it to form a round ball about ½ inch (10 mm) in diameter, tapering down at the base as diagram 1.

Cut a 2 inch (5 cm) diameter circle of light green crêpe paper, place the centre over the top of the cotton wool ball, draw the edges down smoothly all round, and bind tightly underneath with thread or wire (diagram 2).

Cut a piece of white crêpe with grain as arrowed (diagram 3). Trim the top edge with pinking shears, then stretch the upper half of the paper fully, to form a frill (page 8). Glue the strip very loosely round the centre, gathering in the lower edge so that it circles the green ball twice, the top edge of the strip ½–¾ inch (15–20 mm) below the top of the centre (diagram 4): bind tightly with thread or wire (as diagram).

Petals: Trace the pattern and make a template (page 8). Cut five *double* petals as described on page 9, either in two shades of the same colour, or the same shade, and bond together (see page 9).

Paler side uppermost, place a petal on a flat surface. Take second petal and spread a thin line of adhesive *behind* the left-hand edge, below x: then glue over the right-hand edge of the first petal, beginning at the bottom and positioning the corner as indicated by the broken line – twisting the petal slightly on the way up, so that the overlap is the same width (about ⅛ inch – 3 mm) all the way, tapering off just below the widest point of the petals. Join a third petal to the second in the same way, followed by the remaining ones. Then glue the left-hand edge of the first petal over the last one, to form a circle.

Spread adhesive round the base of the centre, then gently lower the stem

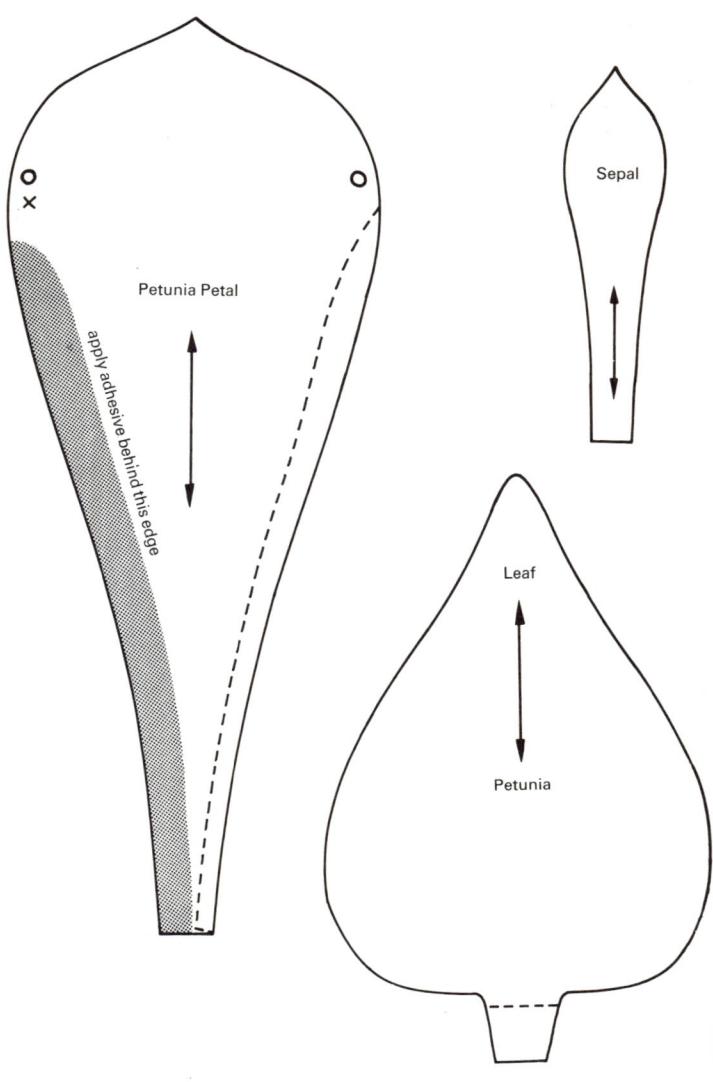

Petunia Petal

apply adhesive behind this edge

Sepal

Leaf

Petunia

through the cone of petals, until the lower edges of the petals and centre are level: pinch together.

Sepals: Make a template, cut five sepals in light green crêpe and glue them evenly round the flower, behind the petals. Then bind the base and stem as directed on page 10.

Leaves: Make a template, and cut one double leaf. Bond together, then apply adhesive below the broken line, and wrap round the stem, about 1½ inches (40 mm) below the flower.

Stroke the sepals (page 8) to curl them round and down. Stretch each petal between o's: then work round again, cupping from behind (page 8) to curve the petals round and back as illustrated. Then carefully frill the outer edges. Cup the lower half of the leaf from behind and stroke the tip to curl it over slightly.

Frilly Pin-cushion Flowers

With that most unusual centre, "pin-cushion flower" is such an apt name for the scabious! If you haven't a very pale blue crêpe for the centre and first round of petals, substitute white.

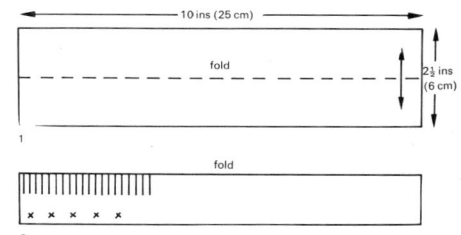

PIN-CUSHION (SCABIOUS)

Materials: Mid blue crêpe paper for main petals
Pale blue crêpe paper for inner petals *(optional)*
White crêpe paper for centre
Light green crêpe paper for centre
Olive green crêpe paper for sepals and stem
Soft-ply face tissues
Plastic-covered garden wire
Fabric adhesive or rubber cement

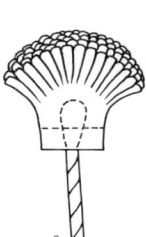

Stem and centre: Bend a 24 inch (60 cm) length of garden wire in half. Twist and glue a 1 inch (25 mm) square of white crêpe paper over and round the bend. Then bind the double wire with strips of folded face tissue, as described on page 10.

Cut two pieces of white crêpe with grain as arrowed (diagram 1). Then cut two more pieces each in pale blue and light green. Make each piece into a folded fringe strip (page 9) as diagram 2, snipping the folded edge closely to a depth of ½ inch (15 mm). Glue a blue strip on top of a green strip, along the lower edge and then glue a white strip over the blue. Repeat with the remaining three strips.

White inside, wrap first one strip, followed by the second, round the top ¾ inch (20 mm) of the stem: keep the lower edges level, but pinch them in so that gradually the top becomes domed, as diagram 3.

Petals: Trace the three patterns and make templates (page 8).

Cut a piece of pale blue crêpe with grain as arrowed (diagram 4). Fold in half, as indicated: place the centre petal pattern at one end, base against the fold, and fold the strip concertina-wise *along* the grain, the same width as the petal. Holding tightly together, cut round the curved top of the petal: then open out the concertina folds and cut down between the petals to ½ inch (10 mm) from the fold. Cut away any excess at the end, and then cut along the fold, to make two single strips of petals. Now glue the two strips together again along the lower edge, so that the centre of each top petal falls over the division between a pair underneath. Cup the top area of each petal (page 8).

Glue the double strip of petals round the centre, gathering in slightly to fit, keeping the lower edge of the petals about ⅜ inch (10 mm) above that of the centre (horizontal broken line on diagram 3).

Cut a piece of mid blue crêpe with grain as arrowed (diagram 5). Fold as previously, then using the inner petal pattern, cut and prepare in the same way. Mark the lower edge of the strip at the half-way point on both sides of the paper; then glue the strip round the flower *twice*, using the centre-mark as a guide. Keep the lower edges of centre and inner petals level.

Cut another piece of mid blue crêpe with grain as arrowed (diagram 6). Using the pattern for the outer petals, repeat the directions for the inner petals.

Sepals: Cut a piece of olive green crêpe with grain as arrowed (diagram 7). Make a template and place at one end of the crêpe, then fold concertinawise along the grain, the width of the sepal; cut round the shaped top, open out and

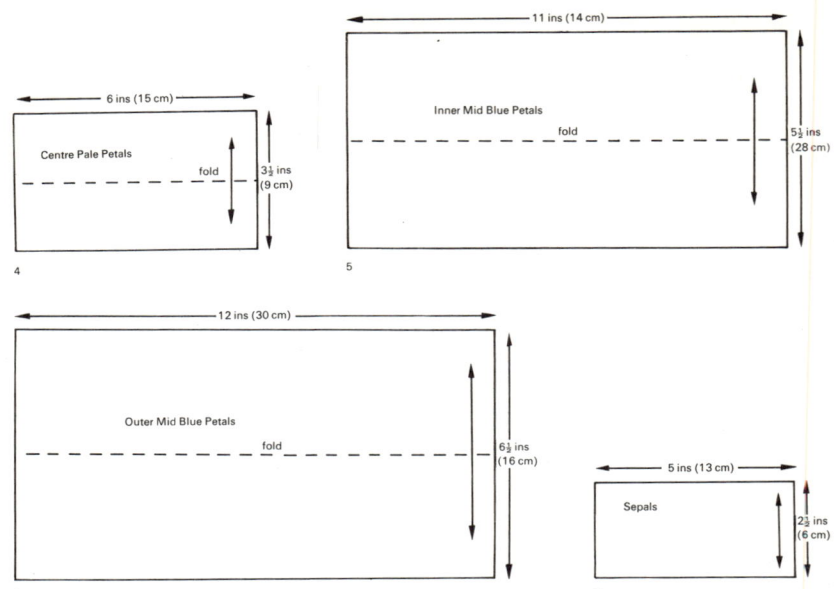

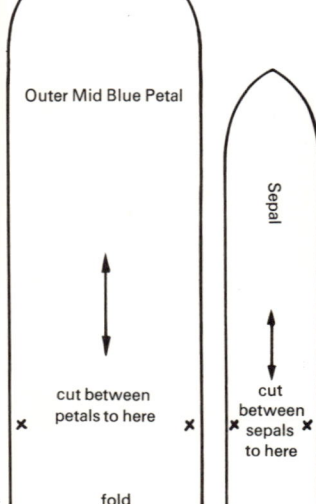

cut down between the sepals to ½ inch (10 mm) from the lower edge. Glue round the flower.

Pad underneath the flower and build up a rounded base with strips of face tissue, as described on page 10. Bind the base and stem as directed on page 10.

Stroke the sepals (page 8) to curl them back and down; gently push the petals down so that the surface of the flower is fairly flat round the domed centre.

Petunias and Pincushion Flowers (pages 53 and 55)

Poppies & Cornflowers

In every old-fashioned wheat field, scarlet poppies and deep blue cornflowers grew. These paper imposters are so spectacular that a few accompanying ears of wheat or barley pale into insignificance beside them!

Scarlet Poppies

Make your outsize corn poppies in brilliant scarlet and orange – adding black markings on the petals if you want oriental poppies instead. Or make stunning opium poppies in lavender, lilac, pink, purple and crimson: or begin with green centres, criss-crossed and surrounded by yellow, with orange, yellow or white petals – for a display of iceland poppies.

Materials: Red or orange crêpe paper for petals
Black crêpe paper for centre
Olive green crêpe paper for stem
Soft-ply face tissues
Thick white embroidery or crochet cotton, dishcloth yarn or fine string for centre
Plastic-covered garden wire
Sewing thread or fine wire
Thin split bamboo garden stakes 18 inches (45 cm) long
Cotton wool
Adhesive tape
Fabric adhesive or rubber cement

POPPY

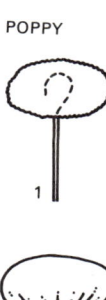

Stem and centre: Cut a 9 inch (23 cm) length of garden wire, turn over ½ inch (15 mm) at one end and hook it through some cotton wool: then wrap and glue the cotton wool around to form a flattish ball about 1½ inches (40 mm) in diameter (diagram 1).

Cut a 5 inch (13 cm) circle of black crêpe paper, stretch the centre slightly, place it over the top of the cotton wool ball and draw the edges down very smoothly all round. Make sure it is quite spherical and bind tightly underneath with thread or wire (diagram 2).

Cut four 5 inch (13 cm) lengths of white cotton, yarn or string. Glue the end of one piece under the centre (x on diagram 2); take it up over the top and down again, glueing the other end at the opposite side of the stalk. Repeat with a second piece, crossing the first exactly in the middle (secure with a tiny spot of adhesive). Add the remaining pieces between the first two. Bind round over the ends of cotton with a narrow piece of crêpe (diagram 3).

Cut five pieces of black crêpe with grain as arrowed (diagram 4). Fold each in half, as indicated, then snip the folded edges closely, to ½ inch from the lower (cut) edge, forming a fringe (diagram 5).

One after another, glue the strips loosely round the centre, with the top edge of the fringe about an inch (25 mm) higher than the centre.

Poppies and Cornflowers (pages 59 and 61)

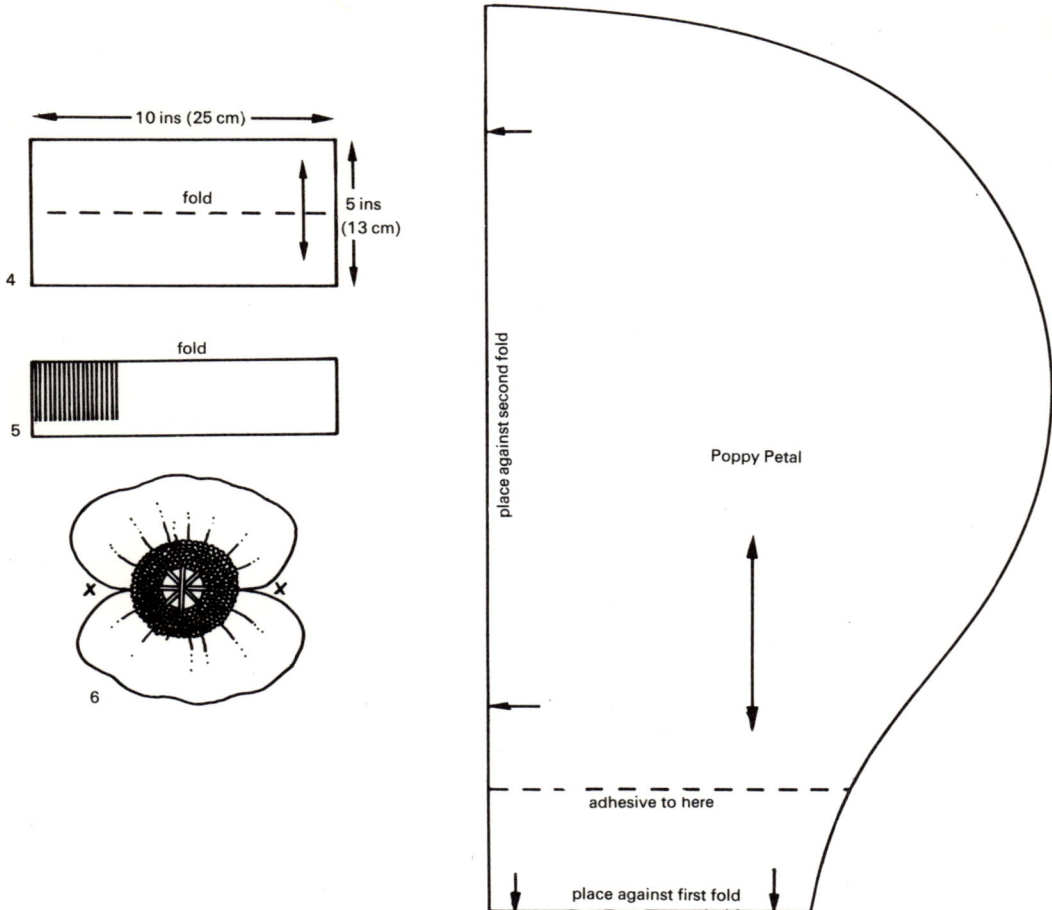

Petals: Trace the pattern and make a template (page 8). Then cut eight *double* petals (page 9) in red or orange crêpe, folded as indicated on the pattern – first in half *across* the grain and then *along* it. Open out the *second* fold only – then cup the centre of each petal (page 8), and frill the edges (page 8).

Spread adhesive generously over the base of one petal: then glue it under the centre, gathering in with the fingertips so that the bunched base of the petal extends half-way round the centre. Add a second petal in the same way, so that it surrounds the other half of the centre (diagram 6). Fix two more petals round the flower, placing them opposite each other, but with their centres *between* the first two (at x on diagram 6). Glue the next pair directly behind the first pair and the final two behind the second pair.

Tape the wire stem securely alongside one end of a thin stick.

Cut a face tissue into four long strips and use to pad and build up the rounded base of the flower, as described on page 10. Then bind the base and stem as directed on page 10.

Field Cornflowers

There are some very pretty cultivated cornflowers in pale blue, soft pinks and pure white. A vase of these would be particularly attractive because the dramatic contrast between the black centres and pale petals is intensified. A few buds help to show off the characteristically shaped base of the flower.

Materials: Cornflower blue crêpe paper for petals (or as above)
Black crêpe paper for centre
White crêpe paper for centre
Olive green crêpe paper for leaves and stem
Soft-ply face tissues
Plastic-covered garden wire
Fine soft wire
Matt surface adhesive tape (optional)
Fabric adhesive or rubber cement

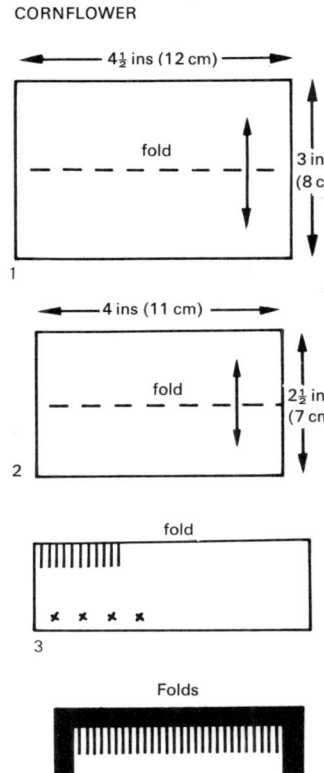

CORNFLOWER

Stem and centre: Cut a 10 inch (25 cm) length of garden wire, turn over ¼ inch (5 mm) at one end, then twist and glue a 1 inch (25 mm) square of black crêpe paper over and round it.

Cut two pieces of black crêpe (grain as arrows, diagram 1) and one piece of white crêpe (grain as arrows, diagram 2). Make each into a folded fringe strip (page 9) as diagram 3, snipping the folded edge closely to a depth of ½ inch (15 mm). Glue the two black strips together with the white strip on top, lower edges level and the black extending equally at either end, as diagram 4.

With the white inside, glue round the top ½ inch (15 mm) of the stem, as diagram 5.

Petals: Trace the pattern and make a template (page 8). Then cut twenty-four *pairs* of petals, joined at the base (see fold on pattern).

Cut a 3 inch (8 cm) length of fine wire, and bend it in half. Link eight petals over the wire, pushing the folds close together so that they are held in the loop: twist the wire tightly underneath to secure. Make up two more clusters in the same way.

Put a dab of adhesive near the base of one cluster; then press it against the black centre, half-way down the side—just below the base of the cuts (x in diagram 5). Glue the other two clusters evenly round the centre in the same

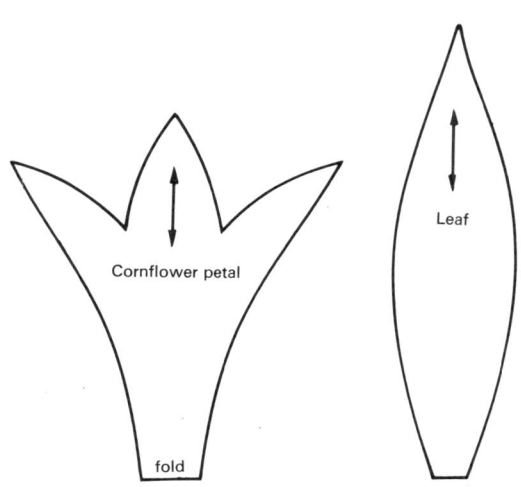

Cornflower petal

Leaf

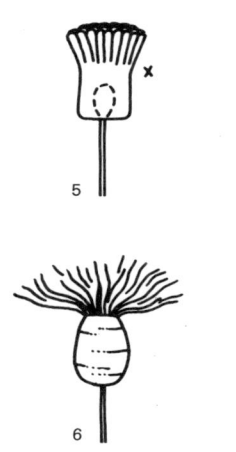

way. Bring the wires neatly down and draw together below the centre, around the stem. Tape round the wires, just below the petals, to hold firmly in place.
Base: Use two strips of face tissue to pad underneath the flower, as described on page 10, and build up a smoothly rounded shape as diagram 6. Then bind the stem with strips of folded tissue padding (page 10). Finally, bind the base and stem with green crêpe, as directed on page 10.
Leaves: Make a template and cut two leaves in olive green crêpe. Glue one each side of the stem and stroke the upper half (page 8) to curl them over slightly as illustrated.
Bud: Make up a stem and *one* cluster of eight pairs of petals, as directed for the flower. Glue the lower ½ inch (15 mm) of the petals to the covered top of the stem.

Build up the rounded base and pad the stem with strips of face tissue, as for the flower. Then bind with olive green crêpe, and add a pair of leaves as before.

Roses all the way

Always a favourite—it's a happy coincidence that paper roses are quick, easy—and very spectacular—to make.

The Classic Rose

Matterhorn—Champs Elysees—Vienna Charm

A combination of strains produced the large hybrid tea rose. The subtle colouring of the petals makes Duplex paper (page 6) an obvious choice for roses. But you can bond two single crêpes together (page 9). Or, for delicate petals, use single crêpe.

Materials: Duplex or single crêpe papers in:
Pale/deep cream or white and pale yellow
Red/deep red or scarlet and wine
Yellow/deep yellow or buttercup and golden
Olive green crêpe paper (single weight) for stem
Deep olive/forest green Duplex for leaves
Soft-ply face tissues
Plastic-covered garden wire
Fine soft wire
Solid stick adhesive (only if not using Duplex crêpe)
Fabric adhesive or rubber cement

All the roses are basically the same but, beginning with the opening buds, extra petals are added for the more fully developed red and yellow versions. Make the stems longer or shorter as required; these are 8 inches (20 cm).

Stem and centre: To begin the **basic centre**, cut an 8 inch (20 cm) length of garden wire, and turn over 3/8 inch (10 mm) at one end, as diagram 1. Cut a piece of petal-coloured crêpe paper about 2 inches (5 cm) by 1 inch (25 mm) wide (grain running lengthwise): fold in half across the grain, snip the fold as diagram 2, and then hook the wire through (diagram 3). Roll and glue the

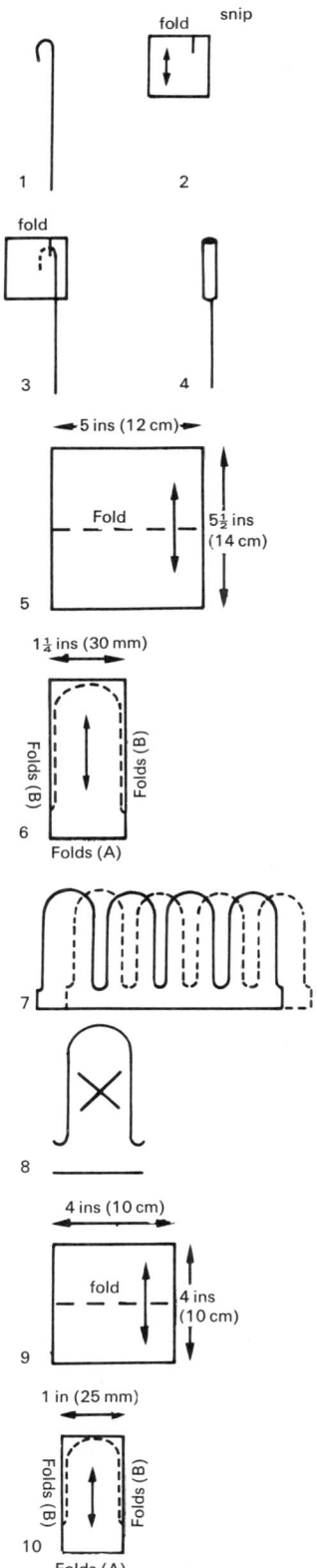

CLASSIC ROSE – HYBRID TEA

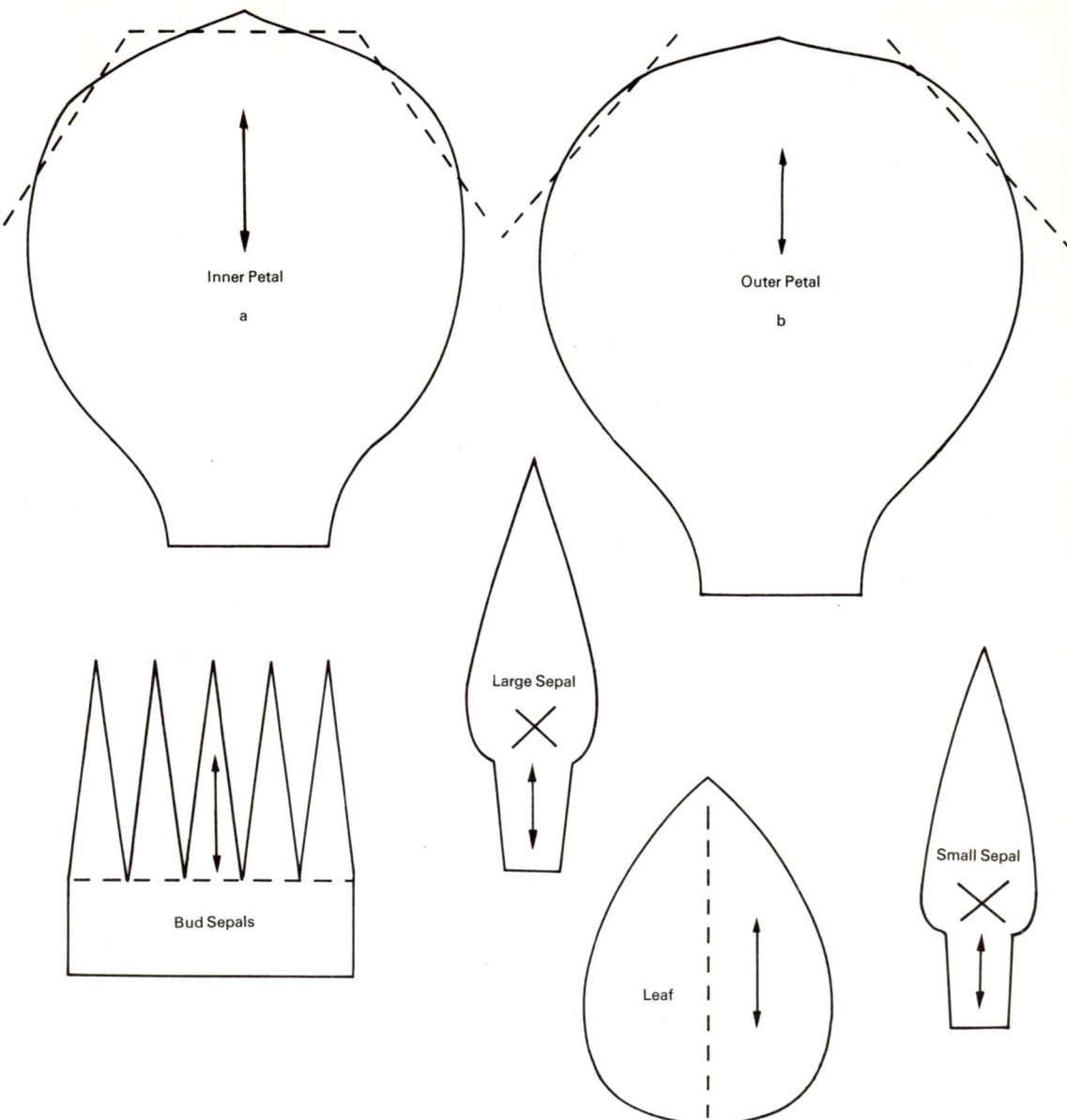

paper tightly round the wire, pinching neatly together (diagram 4).

Cut a piece of petal-coloured Duplex (or cut two shades of single-weight crêpe and bond together—see page 9) with grain as arrowed (diagram 5). Fold in half across the grain, as indicated; then concertina-wise at $1\frac{1}{4}$ inch (30 mm) intervals, along the grain. Cut as indicated by the broken line on diagram 6. Open out folds B and then cut along fold A, making two single strips. Turn one over, so that the paler side of the paper is uppermost on both strips, and glue lightly together again along the lower edge, positioning so that each top petal falls directly between two underneath (diagram 7).

Pale side up, cup each petal very fully (page 8)—as x on diagram 8. Glue the strip round the top of the stem, over the paper foundation. Wrap the first few petals round quite tightly, but towards the end roll the strip more loosely, to prevent the petals being crushed. Pinch the lower edge firmly together.

Matterhorn: Pure, Creamy White

Petals: Trace the inner petal pattern (A), ignoring the broken lines, and make a template (page 8). For the **lower cream rose**, cut five Duplex petals (or, if using two shades of single crêpe, cut *double* petals, as described on page 9, and bond together). Paler side up, cup each petal – fairly low down – and then curl back the tip at the centre, and the top corners, as described on page 8.

Glue three petals evenly round the centre, each half-overlapping the previous one. Then, for the lower rose – which is a little more open than the other – glue the two remaining petals on opposite sides of the bud, behind the first three.

Sepals: Make a template, and cut five *small sepals* in green Duplex (or in light-weight crêpe, using either a single thickness, or cutting each sepal double and bonding together). Stretch slightly at X, and glue evenly round the base.

Bind the stem *twice* with strips of folded face tissue, as described on page 10, to make a double thickness of padding. Then bind the base and stem as directed on page 10. Stroke the tips of the sepals (page 8) so that they curl back as illustrated.

Make the **upper cream rose** in exactly the same way, but cut the stem wire 12 inches (30 cm) long, and prepare only three inner petals (A); glue them around the centre as directed, omitting the final two. Use the *larger* sepal pattern; stretch at X, but do not curl back as before, allowing them to stand up, a little away from the petals, as illustrated. Pad the stem, but stop $4\frac{1}{2}$ inches (11 cm) from the bottom of the wire.

Bind the base and padded stem with green crêpe, then place the remaining wire alongside the stem of the shorter rose, bottoms level, and bind the lower $4\frac{1}{2}$ inches (11 cm) tightly together, reinforcing securely at the join.

Champs-Elysees: Rich, Deep Red

Petals: For the **red rose**, begin with the basic centre: then prepare four inner petals (A) as for the cream buds. Glue evenly round the centre, each half-overlapping the previous one.

Make a template from the outer petal pattern (B). Cut five in Duplex crêpe or your alternative, and prepare as before, cupping well, fairly low down, and rolling the top corners back as indicated by the broken lines. Glue evenly round the rose, lower edges level with those of the first round.

Sepals: Continue as for the lower cream rose, glueing five small sepals round the base of the flower, then padding and binding the stem and stroking the sepals down.

Tiny bud: Repeat the method for the basic centre, but adapted slightly, as follows: cut the stem 7 inches (18 cm) long and prepare the centre petals from a 4 inch (10 cm) square of crêpe (diagram 9), folded in half across the grain, and then at 1 inch (25 mm) intervals along it (diagram 10).

Sepals: Make a template and cut in green Duplex or single-weight crêpe. Spread adhesive below the broken line and glue evenly round the base, gathering in neatly and smoothing with the fingertips.

Pad the stem with face tissue once only. Then bind with green crêpe, halting $3\frac{1}{2}$ inches (9 cm) from the bottom and placing alongside the lower $3\frac{1}{2}$ inches (9 cm) of the stem of the main rose. Continue binding tightly together, reinforcing securely at the join.

Vienna Charm: Glowing Golden Yellow

Petals: For the full-blown **golden rose**, begin with the basic centre, then add four inner petals (A) as for the red rose, followed by five outer petals (B). Prepare six more outer petals; glue these evenly round behind the previous set, keeping the lower edge level at the centre of each petal, but allowing the corners to curve up at each side so that this round of petals opens out more.
Sepals: Continue as for the lower cream rose.
Cream roses – leaf spray:
Stalks: Cut a 9 inch (23 cm) length of garden wire for the main stalk, two 8 inch (20 cm) lengths of fine soft wire for the upper side stalks, and two 6 inch (15 cm) lengths of fine soft wire for the lower side stalks.

Beginning with a neatly pointed tip (see page 10), bind all five wires separately. Then place the two longer side stalks one each side of the main stalk with the ends level and, starting $3\frac{1}{2}$ inches (9 cm) below the tip of the main stalk, bind all three neatly together to the bottom. Place the two shorter side stalks one each side of the main stalk with the ends level and, starting 5 inches (13 cm) below the tip of the main stalk, bind together for $\frac{1}{2}$ inch (15 mm). Place the remaining stalks level in the same way and bind to the bottom; reinforce at the join and double-bind the final section.
Leaves: Make a template and cut five leaves with jagged edges (see page 11) in Duplex crêpe; or bond two pieces of single-weight crêpe together; or just cut in single thickness crêpe. Glue a leaf over each stalk, as directed on page 11.
Red rose and bud – leaf spray:
Stalks: Cut an 8 inch (20 cm) length of garden wire for the main stalk and two $6\frac{1}{2}$ inch (16 cm) lengths of fine soft wire for the side stalks.

Beginning with a neatly pointed tip (see page 10), bind all three wires separately. Then place one fine stalk at each side of the main stalk with the ends level and, starting 4 inches (10 cm) below the tip of the main stalk, bind neatly together to the bottom.

Place the stalk of the leaf spray alongside the flower stem and bind the bottom 3 inches (8 cm) together. Reinforce at the join, then double-bind.
Leaves: Cut three leaves and glue into position as for the cream roses leaf spray, curving the wires back so that the leaves curl round as illustrated.
Golden rose – leaf sprays:
Stalks: For the upper leaves, cut an 8 inch (20 cm) length of garden wire for the main stalk and two $6\frac{1}{2}$ inch (16 cm) lengths of fine wire for side stalks.

Beginning with a neatly pointed tip (see page 10), bind all three wires separately. Then place one fine stalk at each side of the main stalk with the ends level and, starting $3\frac{1}{2}$ inches (9 cm) below the tip of the main stalk, bind neatly together to the bottom.

Place the stalk of the leaf spray alongside the flower stem, and bind the bottom $3\frac{1}{2}$ inches (9 cm) tightly together, reinforcing at the join.

Make the lower spray in exactly the same way, but cut the main stalk 7 inches (18 cm) long, and the two side stalks $5\frac{1}{2}$ inches (14 cm) long. Then place alongside the stem, and bind the bottom $2\frac{1}{2}$ inches (6 cm) together, reinforcing as before and then double-binding the final section.
Leaves: Cut six leaves and stick into position as for the cream roses leaf spray, curving the wires back so that the leaves curl round as illustrated.

Roses all the Way (pages 63 to 75)
Sunflowers and Peonies (pages 76 and 81)

Cabbage Rose and Bud

Lovingly painted by Redouté, the famous Rose of Provence is one of the oldest varieties. This is a *rosa centifolia*—which means it has a hundred petals. My paper version has a hundred and four!

- Materials: Deep pink crêpe paper for centre petals
  Medium pink crêpe paper for inner petals
  Pale pink crêpe paper for outer petals (optional)
  Olive green crêpe paper for sepals and stem
  Deep olive/forest green Duplex crêpe paper for leaves
  Soft-ply face tissues
  Golden-yellow raffia
  Plastic-covered garden wire : Fine soft wire
  Sewing thread (optional)
  Solid stick adhesive (if not using Duplex crêpe)
  Fabric adhesive or rubber cement

Stem and centre: Cut a 9 inch (23 cm) length of garden wire and five 2 inch (5 cm) lengths of raffia. Turn over $\frac{3}{8}$ inch (10 mm) at one end of the wire (diagram 1) and hook over the centre of the raffia (diagram 2). Bend the hook back and bind the raffia tightly with thread or wire; then trim the cut ends level (diagram 3). Finally bind round the looped wire and raffia with a strip of deep pink crêpe, as diagram 4.

Centre petals: Cut a piece of deep pink crêpe (grain as arrows, diagram 5). Fold in half across the grain, as indicated; then concertina-wise at $1\frac{1}{2}$ inch (40 mm) intervals, along the grain and cut as indicated by the broken line on diagram 6. Open out folds B, and then cut along fold A, making two single strips. Turn one over and stick them lightly together again along the lower edge, positioning so that each top petal falls directly over the division between two underneath (diagram 7). Cup each petal (page 8) low down at large X (diagram 8) on the *wrong* side of the crêpe.

Wrap the strip round the raffia centre, glueing the lower edge over the paper foundation: wrap the first few petals round quite tightly; then gradually roll the strip round more loosely, gathering the lower edge in neatly with the fingertips.

Inner petals: Cut two pieces of medium pink crêpe as diagram 9; and two more pieces as diagram 10. Make up into four strips of overlapped petals, as previously described (diagrams 6 and 7). Cup the first two ($2\frac{1}{4}$ inches – 5·7 cm – deep) sets of petals as X on diagram 8, but cup the second two ($2\frac{1}{2}$ inches – 6·5 cm – deep) sets of petals *twice*, first low down, and then above as X's on diagram 11. Stick the first two sets of medium pink petals round the deep pink ones, letting the lower edge become looser as necessary; and pinching in the base as before.

Pad underneath the flower with strips of face tissue, as described on page 10, to prevent the remaining petals slipping down as you glue them into place. Now fix the second two strips of petals round as before.

Outer petals: Trace the pattern (ignoring broken lines) and make a template (page 8). Cut twenty-four petals in pale pink (or medium pink) crêpe.

Dahlias and Chrysanthemums (pages 83 and 84)
Christmas Roses and Ivy (pages 86, 88 and 89)

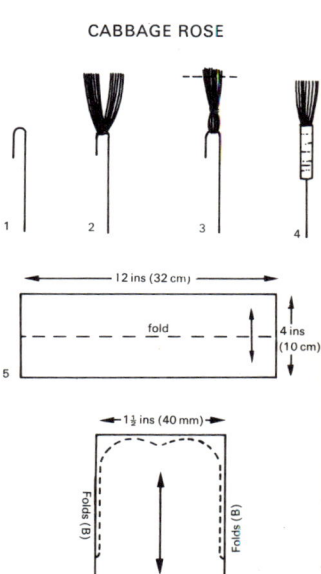

CABBAGE ROSE

71

CABBAGE ROSE

Divide into three sets of eight. Cup the first two sets of eight petals well, on the wrong side of the paper; then cup the remaining eight *very* fully on the *right* side of the crêpe. Curl back the top corners of these last eight (page 8).

Glue the first set of eight uncurled petals equally round the rose, each half-overlapping the previous one. Then glue the second set of uncurled petals round, followed by the final eight curled ones.

Use more strips of face tissue padding to form the rounded base of the flower and to bind the stem two or three times, to thicken it (see page 10).

Sepals: Make a template: cut once in olive green crêpe, spread adhesive below the broken line, and glue evenly round the base.

Bind the base and stem as directed on page 10 Then stroke the tips of the sepals (page 8) so that they curl back slightly.

The bud: Follow the above directions for the stem, raffia centre and deep pink petals.

Bud sepals: Make a template; cut five in olive green crêpe, cup each at X and then stick evenly round the bud.

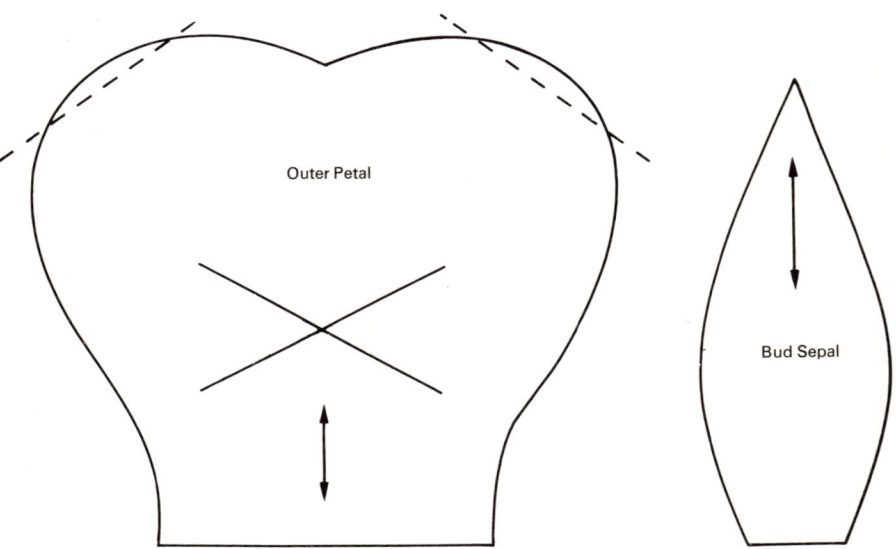

Outer Petal

Bud Sepal

Use strips of face tissue padding to form the rounded base of the bud and thicken the stem, as for the flower. Bind the base and stem as before, but pause 2 inches (5 cm) from the end; place the remainder of the stem alongside the stem of the flower with the bud-stem 2 inches (5 cm) above the bottom of the flower-stem and continue binding the two together to the end, reinforcing well at the join.

The leaf spray: Cut a 9 inch (23 cm) length of garden wire for the main stalk and two 8 inch (20 cm) lengths of fine soft wire for the side stalks.

Beginning each with a pointed tip (see page 10), bind all three wires separately. Then place a fine wire stalk at each side of the main stalk with the ends level and, starting 4 inches (10 cm) below the tip of the main stalk, bind all three neatly together, pausing 4 inches (10 cm) from the end. Place the remainder of the stalks alongside the flower stem, and bind the bottom 4 inches (10 cm) tightly together.

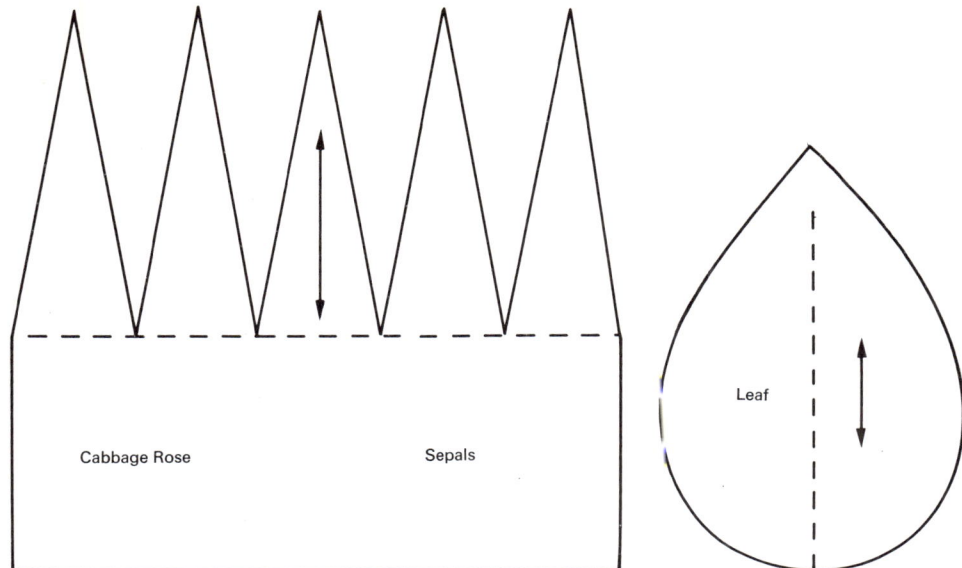

Cabbage Rose   Sepals   Leaf

Leaves: Make a template, and cut three leaves with jagged edges (see page 11) in olive green Duplex crêpe. If you do not have this, bond two pieces of singleweight crêpe together (page 9) or just cut in single thickness crêpe. Glue a leaf over each stalk as described on page 11. Then curve the wires back so that they curl round as illustrated.

Floribunda Cluster

The beauty of the floribunda and grandiflora varieties is the combination of flower heads from buds through to full-bloom all on one main stem.

Materials: Pale pink crêpe paper for petals
Pale yellow crêpe paper for petals
Dark green crêpe paper for sepals and stems
Dark green Duplex crêpe paper for leaves (optional)
Soft-ply face tissues
Plastic-covered garden wire
Fine soft wire
Solid stick adhesive
Fabric adhesive or rubber cement

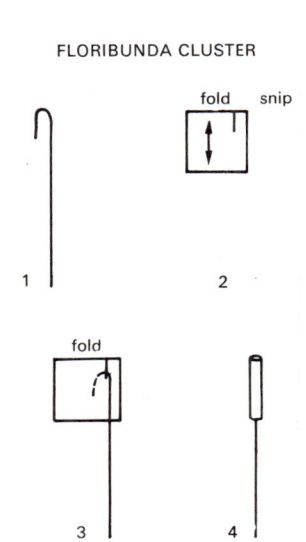

FLORIBUNDA CLUSTER

Method: The complete cluster is made up of three separate stems, each composed of two full flowers, a bud, and a spray of leaves. The main leaf stalk, the bud stem and one flower stem are all 8 inches (20 cm) long; the other flower stem is 9 inches (23 cm) long.

Stem and centre: To make a fully-open rose, cut a piece of garden wire 8 inches (20 cm) or 9 inches (23 cm) long, as explained above. Turn over ⅜ inch (10 mm) at one end (diagram 1). Cut a piece of pink crêpe paper about 2 inches (5 cm) by 1 inch (25 mm) wide (grain running lengthways): fold in half across the grain, snip the fold as diagram 2, and then hook the wire through (diagram 3). Roll and glue the paper tightly round the wire (diagram 4).

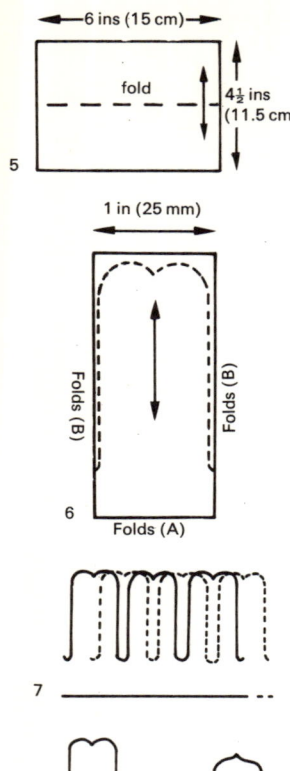
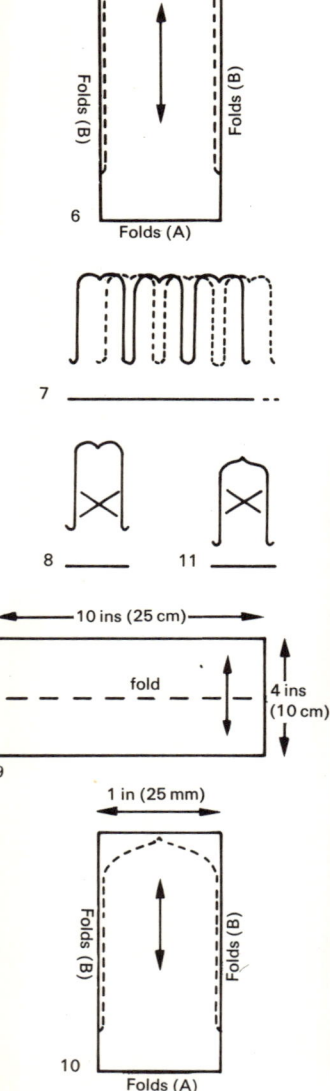

Centre petals: Cut a piece of pink crêpe (grain as arrows, diagram 5). Fold in half across the grain as indicated; then concertina-wise at 1 inch (25 mm) intervals, along the grain. Cut as indicated by the broken line on diagram 6. Open out folds B and then cut along fold A, making two single strips. Turn one over, then stick lightly together again along the lower edge, positioning so that each top petal falls directly over the division between two underneath (diagram 7). Cup the lower half of each petal (page 8) at X (diagram 8) on the *wrong* side of the crêpe.

Glue the strip round the top of the stem, over the paper foundation; wrap the first few petals round quite tightly and then gradually roll the strip a little more loosely, to prevent the petals being crushed, gathering the lower edge in neatly with the fingertips.

Inner petals: Trace pattern A, ignoring the broken lines, and make a template (page 8). Cut four *double* petals, one side pink and the other pale yellow, as described on page 9; then bond together (see page 9). With the yellow side uppermost, cup each petal and curl back first the tip at the centre, then the top corners, as directed on page 8. Glue the four petals evenly round the centre, each half-overlapping the previous one.

Outer petals: Make a template from pattern B and cut five petals in yellow crêpe. Cup these (on the right side) and then curl the top corners as indicated by the broken lines. Glue evenly round the flower as for the inner petals.

Pad the stem with a strip of face tissue as described on page 10, to a point 4 inches (10 cm) from the bottom.

Sepals: Make a template, and cut in dark green crêpe. Spread adhesive below the broken line, and glue evenly round the base, gathering neatly, and smoothing with the fingertips.

Bind the base and padded section of the stem as directed on page 10. Stroke the tips of the sepals (page 8) so that they curl back.

Partially opened rose: follow the above directions, omitting the five pale yellow outer petals.

The bud: Cut an 8 inch (20 cm) length of garden wire, and prepare the tip as for the full flower (diagrams 1–4).

Cut a piece of pink crêpe (grain as arrows, diagram 9). Fold in half across the grain as indicated; then concertina-wise at 1 inch (25 mm) intervals, along the grain. Cut as indicated by the broken line on diagram 10. Now prepare the double strip of petals as for the centre of the flower, but cup the *centre* of each petal, as X on diagram 11.

Glue the strip round the top of the stem, as before. Then pad the stem, add the sepals and bind as for the flower. Leave the sepals standing up, close to the petals, as illustrated.

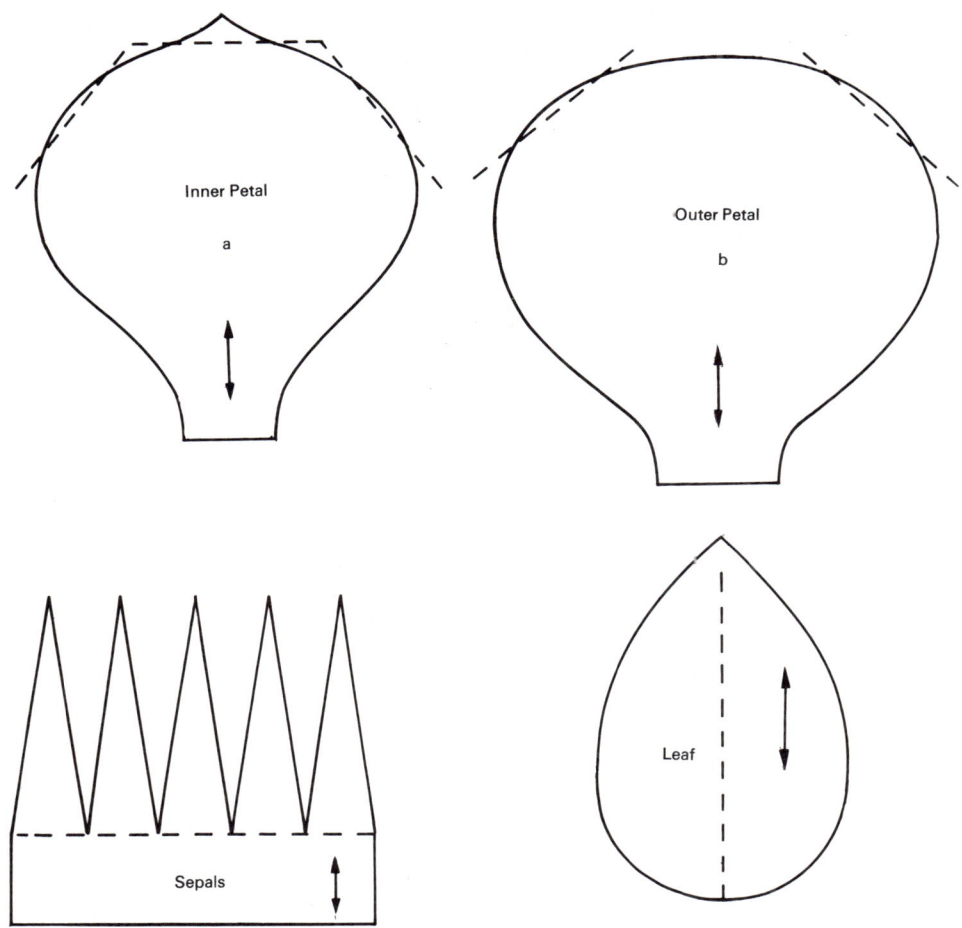

Leaves: Make a template, and cut three leaves with jagged edges (see page 11) in dark green Duplex crêpe (or bond two pieces of single-weight crêpe use single thickness crêpe). Glue a leaf on each stalk (page 11).
To assemble spray: Hold the stems of the two flowers, the bud and the leaf stalk firmly in one hand, the lower ends of all four level. Bind the lower 4 inches (10 cm) tightly together, reinforcing securely at the join.
To assemble the cluster: Hold the stems of the three sprays firmly, lower ends level; then bind the lower 3–3½ inches (8–9 cm) securely together as described for the spray. Arrange the flowers and curve the leaves back.

Sunflower & Peonies

Giant decorations with sensational impact, for festive occasions either indoors or on the patio.

Radiant Sunflower

As some sunflowers go this one's just a baby – though it does measure a foot (30 cm) in diameter, and should be large enough for most needs!

Materials: Buttercup yellow crêpe paper for petals
Brown crêpe paper for stamens
Black crêpe paper for centre
Olive green crêpe paper for sepals and stem
Stiff card
A cork 9 about $1\frac{1}{2}$–2 inches (4–5 cm) long by $\frac{3}{4}$–1 inch (20–25 mm) diameter
2 (or more) pipe cleaners
Pins (1 inch–25 mm)
Thick bamboo cane–about $\frac{3}{8}$–$\frac{1}{2}$ inch (10–15 mm) diameter by 2–3 feet (60–90 cm) long
Solid stick adhesive (optional)
Fabric adhesive or rubber cement

Centre: Cut a 4 inch (10 cm) diameter circle of stiff card. Mark the centre, and then draw concentric circles 1 inch (25 mm), 2 inches (5 cm) and 3 inches (7.5 cm) in diameter, as diagram 1.

Cut about twenty strips of black crêpe paper (grain as arrows, diagram 2). Make into folded fringe strips (page 9) as diagram 3, snipping the folded edge closely to a depth of about $\frac{1}{4}$ inch (5 mm).

Roll up the first strip loosely and brush adhesive liberally over the lower, cut, edges. When dry, brush with more adhesive and glue in the centre of the card circle (diagram 4).

Brush adhesive tickly on to the card, against the base of the central crêpe and extending about $\frac{1}{4}$ inch (10 mm) outwards. Wind a second strip 4 fringe loosely round the first, the fringed top edges touching closely. Take care to prevent the lower edge being pushed in towards the centre; the strip must stand up as straight as possible. Continue adding more strips, still keeping the fringed top edges smooth and close, and avoiding the lower edges closing inwards. Use the marked circles as a guide to keep the rounds in shape.

When about half the strips are in position, you can let the lower edges gradually curve inwards; but not too much or too soon! The angle will increase, until the lower edge of the final strip is about $\frac{1}{4}$ inch (6 mm) inside the rim of the card, with the fringed edge above overlapping about $\frac{1}{4}$ inch (6 mm) outside the rim (diagram 5).

Cut four pieces of brown crêpe (grain as arrows, diagram 6). Fold each strip in half as indicated, but this time snip the *cut* edge fairly closely to a depth of about 1 inch (25 mm) to form a fringe (diagram 7).

Stroke the fringe (page 8) to curl it. Then glue one strip round the centre, stretching it to fit, with the lower edge overlapping the edge of the card about ⅛ inch (3 mm). Turn this excess under and glue to the back of the card (diagram 8). Release any curls of fringe with a pencil or knitting needle.

Glue a second strip round behind the first one, but with the folded lower edge level with the edge of the card; then add the remaining strips in the same way. Release any curled fringe and gently pull the curled strips outwards, so that they don't conceal the centre too much.

Petals: Trace the two patterns and make templates (page 8). Using template A, cut sixteen *double* petals (page 9) in yellow crêpe.

Bond each double petal lightly together at each side, as shaded areas on the pattern (see page 9).

Glue eight petals equally round the centre, spreading adhesive below the broken line, when pressing the petal against the lower half of the brown fringe, the lower edge level with the edge of the card. Glue the remaining eight petals round in the same way, but so that the centre of each new petal falls exactly *between* two petals in the first round.

Base: Cut another circle in card, this time 3¾ inches (9·5 cm) in diameter: mark the centre, then draw a 2½ inch (6 cm) diameter circle, and another, 1½ inches (40 mm) in diameter (diagram 9).

Make a hole at least an inch (25 mm) deep in the narrow end of the cork. Bend two (or more) pipe cleaners in half, then push the bent ends into the hole, until they are firmly wedged (diagram 10 and 11).

Glue the broad end of the cork to the centre of the new circle – securing it with pins as diagram 11. Now glue the back of this circle to the back of the large one.

Cut out and make up sixteen larger petals (B) in double yellow crêpe, exactly as before. Glue eight round the flower, positioned directly behind the *first* round of small petals, but with the lower edge overlapping the edge of the card about ¼ inch (5–6 mm). Turn this excess under and glue. Add the remaining set of eight petals directly behind the *second* round of small petals, overlapping the lower edges and glueing them neatly under, as previously.

Sepals: Make a template, and cut twenty-eight *double* sepals in olive green crêpe, making up as the petals. Glue eight sepals round the back of the flower, one behind each of the last round of large petals – glueing the base of the sepal (below the broken line) over the base of the petal, so that the lower edges of both are level. Glue eight more sepals to the back of the flower, the lower edges level with the larger circle marked on the card, and the tips falling between the sepals in the previous round.

Now glue four sepals equally round the card, the lower edges level with the smaller marked circle, positioned directly behind every second sepal in the first round. Then add another four – between the previous ones, but with the lower edges against the edge of the cork. Glue the final four round the cork itself, ending about half-way down it, and positioned behind a sepal in the second round.

Push the protruding ends of the pipe cleaners firmly into one end of the bamboo cane, wedging them if necessary and leaving just enough space between the top of the cane and the cork to bend the flower head at an angle to the stem. Bind the lower half of the cork and the cane, as directed on page 7: don't stretch the binding around the area between the cork and cane and overlap the layers more closely, to allow for play (I double-bound the joint, lightly glueing the crêpe).

Finally, cup the centre of each sepal (page 8), so that they curve away

SUNFLOWER

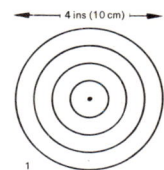

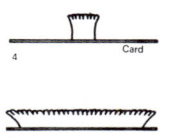

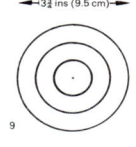

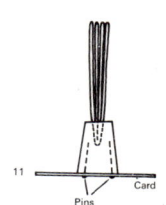

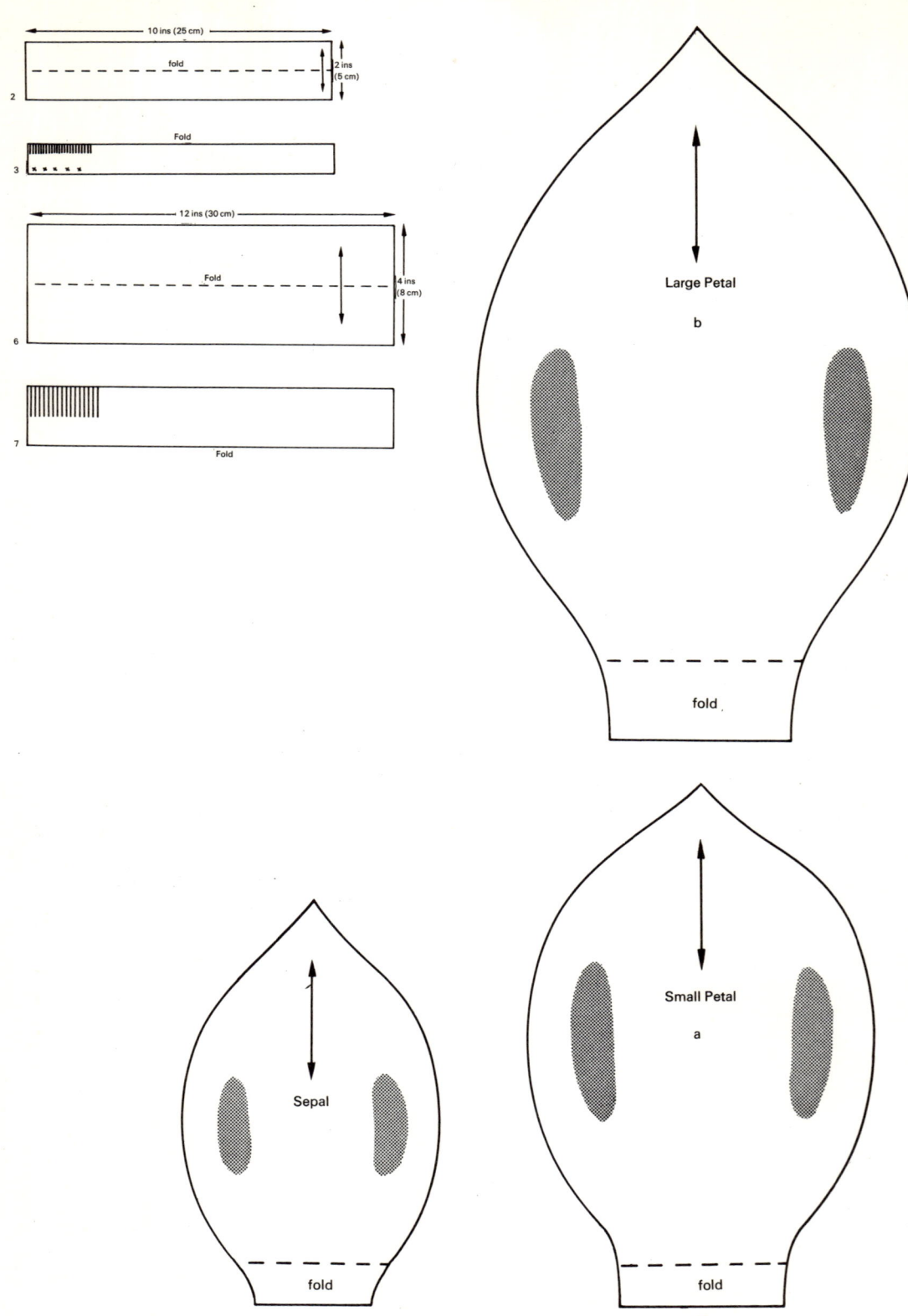

'Kitchenalia Floribunda' (pages 91 and 92)

from the petals – beginning with the outer ones and working towards the stem. Then cup the petals fully, in the same way – working from the outside towards the centre.

Many-petalled Peonies

Gentle explosions of frilly petals, peonies are such theatrical flowers that they steal the limelight in any setting.

Materials: Crêpe paper for petals (deep red, pink or white)
Deep yellow crêpe paper for centre
Olive green crêpe paper for sepals and stem
Lime green soft-ply paper napkin or tissue (or crêpe) for centre
Soft-ply face tissues
Plastic-covered garden wire
Sewing thread or fine wire
Thin garden stakes – 12 inches (30 cm) or longer
Cotton wool
Adhesive tape
Solid stick adhesive
Fabric adhesive or rubber cement

Stem and centre: Cut a 6 inch (15 cm) length of garden wire, turn over ⅜ inch (10 mm) at one end, then wrap and glue cotton wool around it to form a ball just over an inch (25 mm) in diameter (diagram 1).

Cut a 4½ inch (11 cm) diameter circle of lime green paper napkins: place the centre over the top of the cotton wool, draw the edges smoothly down all round and bind tightly underneath with thread or wire (diagram 2). The diameter of the ball should now be about an inch (25 mm).

Cut a piece of bright yellow crêpe paper (grain as arrows, diagram 3). Cut two more pieces of crêpe, one each in bright and deep yellow (grain as arrows, diagram 4). Fold each strip in half as indicated, and then snip the cut edges closely to within ½ inch (10 mm) of the folded lower edge, to form a fine fringe (diagram 5).

Glue the lower edge of the narrower bright yellow strip loosely round the centre, pinching tightly together underneath. Stroke the fringe (page 8) to curl *inwards*, over the centre (diagram 6).

Glue the remaining yellow strips together along the lower edge. With the bright yellow inside, glue round the centre, over the previous strip, pinching underneath as before. Stroke the new fringe, to curl over in the same direction (diagram 6).

Push the tip of a thin garden stake (at least 12 inches – 30 cm – long) close up under the centre, and tape alongside the wire stem.

Petals: Cut two pieces of crêpe for the inner petals (a), 6 inches (15 cm) deep by 9 inches (24 cm) wide with the grain as arrowed on diagram 7(a). Cut two more pieces for the middle petals (b), 8 inches (20 cm) deep by 12 inches

PEONY

Moonbeam Icicalia (page 93)

(30 cm) wide: diagram 7(b). Cut two pieces for the outer petals (c), 10 inches (25 cm) deep by 15 inches (39 cm) wide: diagram 7(c).

Fold each inner petal piece (a) in half as indicated; then fold concertina-wise, at $1\frac{1}{2}$ inch (40 mm) intervals, cut as shown by the broken line on diagram 8(a), making an uneven, wavy top edge, as diagram 9. Open out folds B and cut along fold A – making each double strip into two single ones: then glue each pair lightly together again along the lower edge, positioning so that each top petal falls directly over the division between two underneath (diagram 10). Cup each petal very fully (page 8) as indicated by the broken line on diagram 9.

Glue the lower edge of one petal strip loosely round the centre (lower edges level), gathering in and pinching together neatly underneath. Follow with the second strip.

Fold each middle petal piece (b) in half as indicated; then fold concertina-wise at 2 inch (5 cm) intervals and cut as before, following diagram 8(b). Make up strips of cupped petals, and glue round the flower, as above.

Finally, fold each outer petal piece (c) in half, and fold concertina-wise at $2\frac{1}{2}$ inch (6·5 cm) intervals, cutting as diagram 8(c). Make up strips and glue round the flower as previously.

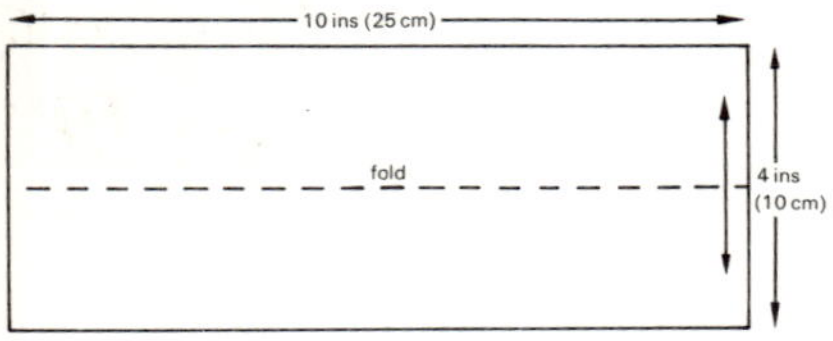

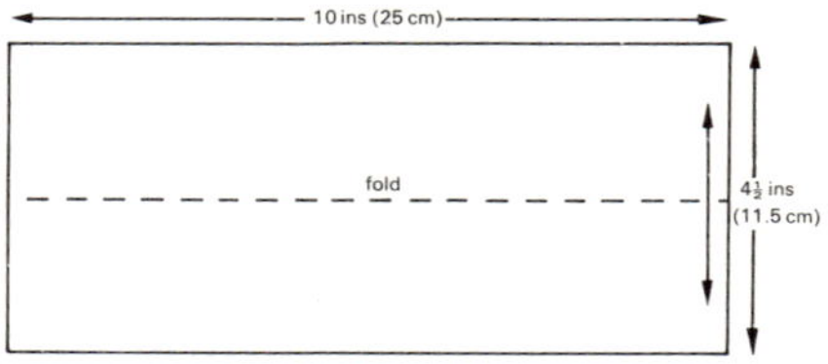

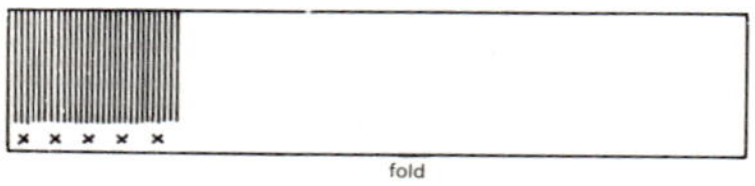

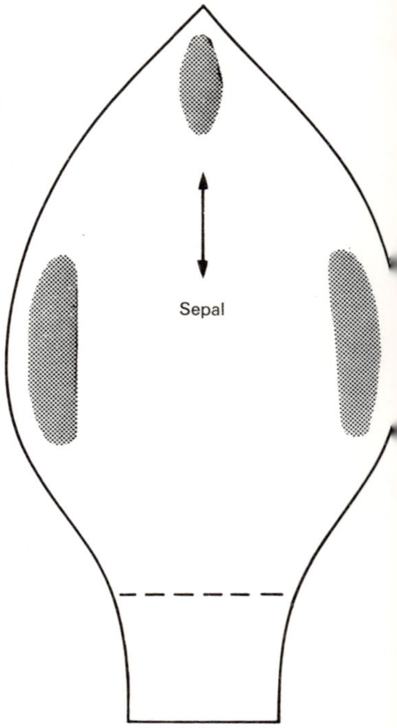

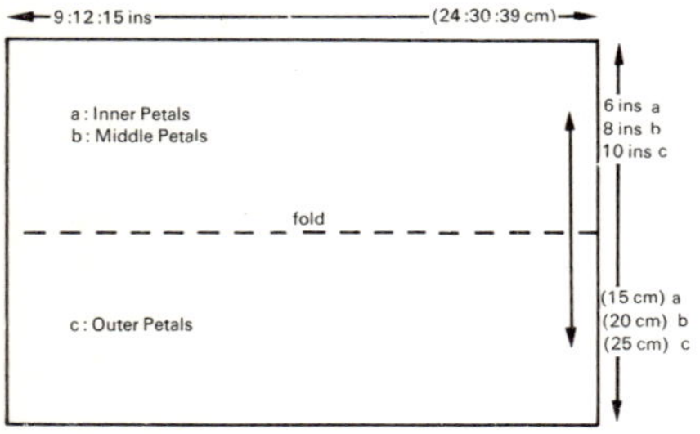

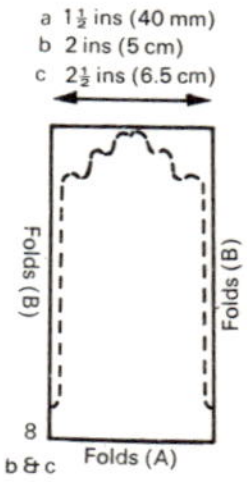

Sepals: Trace the pattern and make a template (page 8). Cut five *double* sepals (page 9) in olive green crêpe, bonding together as shown by shaded areas on the pattern (see page 9). Cup the centre of each sepal, then glue evenly round the base of the flower.

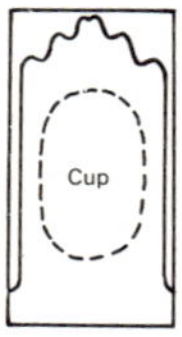

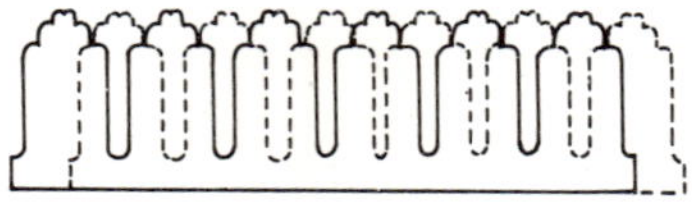

Cut a face tissue into four equal strips and use to pad underneath the centre and form the rounded base of the flower, as described on page 10. Then bind the base and stem as directed on page 10.

Dahlias & Chrysanthemums

Richly glowing shades of yellow, gold, orange, crimson and brown are reflected in the flowers of September.

Colour-shaded Dahlias

I copied these from my mother's garden, trying to capture the wonderfully shaded colour-schemes. Plan out your arrangement, listing the colours in order, working out from the centre – and letter each as shown below. Then you can see at a glance the paper for each section, and follow the directions without confusion.

My choice of colour schemes:

	Inner centre – A	Outer centre – B	Inner petals – C	Outer petals – D
1	lime green	buttercup yellow	orange	bright red
2	medium-yellow	golden yellow	white	claret (wine)
3	light brown	dark brown	buttercup yellow	lemon yellow
4	dark brown	dark brown	golden yellow	orange

Materials: Soft-ply paper napkin or tissue (or crêpe) for inner centre (A)
Crêpe paper for outer centre (B)
Crêpe paper for inner petals (C)
Crêpe paper for outer petals (D)
Olive green crêpe paper for sepals and stem
Soft-ply face tissues
Plastic-covered garden wire
Sewing thread or fine wire
Thin split bamboo garden stakes (12 inches – 30 cm – long)
Cotton wool
Adhesive tape
Fabric adhesive or rubber cement

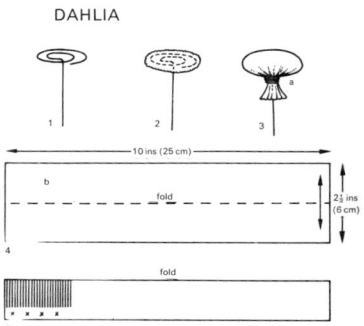

DAHLIA

Stem and inner centre: Cut a 9 inch (23 cm) length of garden wire and curl the top 3 inches (8 cm) round into a flat spiral ¾ inch (20 mm) in diameter, as diagram 1. Wrap a layer of cotton wool smoothly around the spiral, making it about 1 inch (25 mm) in diameter, as diagram 2.

Cut a 4 inch (10 cm) diameter circle of soft-ply napkin or tissue (A) and place over the top of the cotton wool; bring the edges down evenly all round and bind securely with thread or wire underneath (diagram 3).

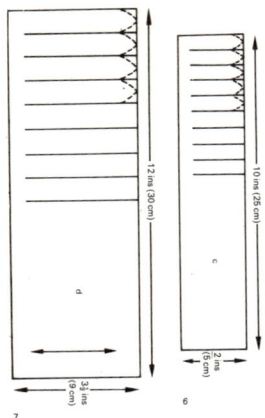

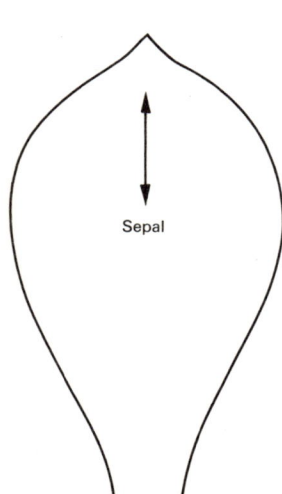

Outer centre: Cut a piece of crêpe paper B (grain as arrows, diagram 4). Make a folded fringe strip (page 9) as diagram 5, snipping the folded edge closely to a depth of ¾ inch (20 mm). Glue the strip loosely round the base of the centre, the top edge of the fringe just above the level of the centre.

Inner petals: Cut three pieces of crêpe C (grain as arrows, diagram 6). Place all the strips together, edges level, and cut at ½ inch (10 mm) intervals to within ½ inch (15 mm) of the lower edge, as diagram 6 (don't compare imperial and metric equivalents!) Then trim the top of each petal to a rounded point, as indicated.

Cut one strip in half, and glue one half on top of the other along the lower edge, so that each upper petal falls centrally over the division between a pair of petals beneath. Glue the two remaining long strips of petals together, in the same way.

Glue the short strip loosely round the fringed centre, gathering the base. Follow with the long strip.

Outer petals: Cut four pieces of crêpe D, as diagram 7. Cut at ¾ inch (15 mm) intervals to within ½ inch (15 mm) of the lower edge, as diagram 7: trim the tops of the petals to rounded points, and then divide the stripe into two pairs and glue each pair together, positioned as before.

Glue each strip round the flower as previously.

Sepals: Trace the pattern and make a template (page 8). Cut five in olive green crêpe, and glue evenly round behind the outer petals.

Tape the wire stem alongside one end of a thin stick.

Use strips of face tissue to pad underneath the centre and form the rounded base of the flower, as described on page 10. Then bind the base and stem as directed on page 10.

Stroke the inner petals (page 8) from behind, so that they curl round and back towards the longer petals beneath. Then stroke the tips only of the outer petals—from the *front*, so that they curl forward. Finally, stroke the tips of the sepals, and slightly cup (page 8) from behind, the curve round and back.

Double Chrysanthemums

The softer and silkier your paper the better, to flatter the multitude of curled petals which are the spectacular beauty of double chrysanthemums.

Materials: Crêpe paper for petals
Olive green crêpe paper for leaves and stem
Soft-ply face tissues
Thin split bamboo garden stakes (12 inches—30 cm—long)
Fabric adhesive or rubber cement

Stem and centre: Twist and glue a 1 inch (25 mm) square of petal-coloured crêpe paper round the tip of a thin garden stake.

Petals: Cut a piece of the same crêpe (grain as arrows, diagram 1). Right side *inside*, fold in half as indicated; then cut the folded edge at ¼ inch (5 mm) intervals, to ⅜–½ inch (10 mm) from the lower edge (diagram 2). Open up the strip and smooth out the fold, so that the paper will curve round in the opposite direction.

Place the strip right side down on a flat surface (diagram 3a), and lay a piece of rounded stick, such as bamboo cane or dowelling, measuring about

½ inch (15 mm) in diameter, over the fold-line (diagram 3b). Now bring one side up, rolling it over the cane or dowelling, and glue the two long edges lightly together, taking care not to re-crease the fold at all: remove the cane or dowelling (diagram 3c).

CHRYSANTHEMUM

Cut three more pieces of paper as diagram 4. Right side *inside*, fold each in half as indicated; place the strips together, absolutely smooth and flat, with edges level, and cut the folded edge as before, but at ⅜ inch (10 mm) intervals, to ⅜–½ inch (10 mm) from the lower edge.

Finally, cut four pieces of paper as diagram 5. Fold, and cut to the same measurements as the last strips.

Open out and prepare all seven strips as diagrams 3a, b and c.

Glue the first, narrowest, strip evenly round the covered top ½ inch (15 mm) of the stick. Pinch the lower edge tightly together while it is still wet. Cut a strip of face tissue and pad round the stick, under the first petal strip, as described on page 10 to form a firm base for the remaining strips.

Now glue one of the three narrower strips loosely round so that the lower edge of this strip is about ¼ inch (5–6 mm) below that of the first one, making the top loops a little higher than those in the centre. Squeeze the lower edge tightly, as before. Add the two remaining narrower strips in the same way, keeping the lower edges level. Then glue one of the four wider strips round, the lower edge not more than ½ inch (12 mm) below that of the previous ones, so that the looped tops remain at the same level. Follow with the three remaining strips, gently smoothing the looped petals upwards to make room for each new strip.

Pad underneath with strips of face tissue, to form the rounded base of the flower, then bind the base and stem as directed on page 10.

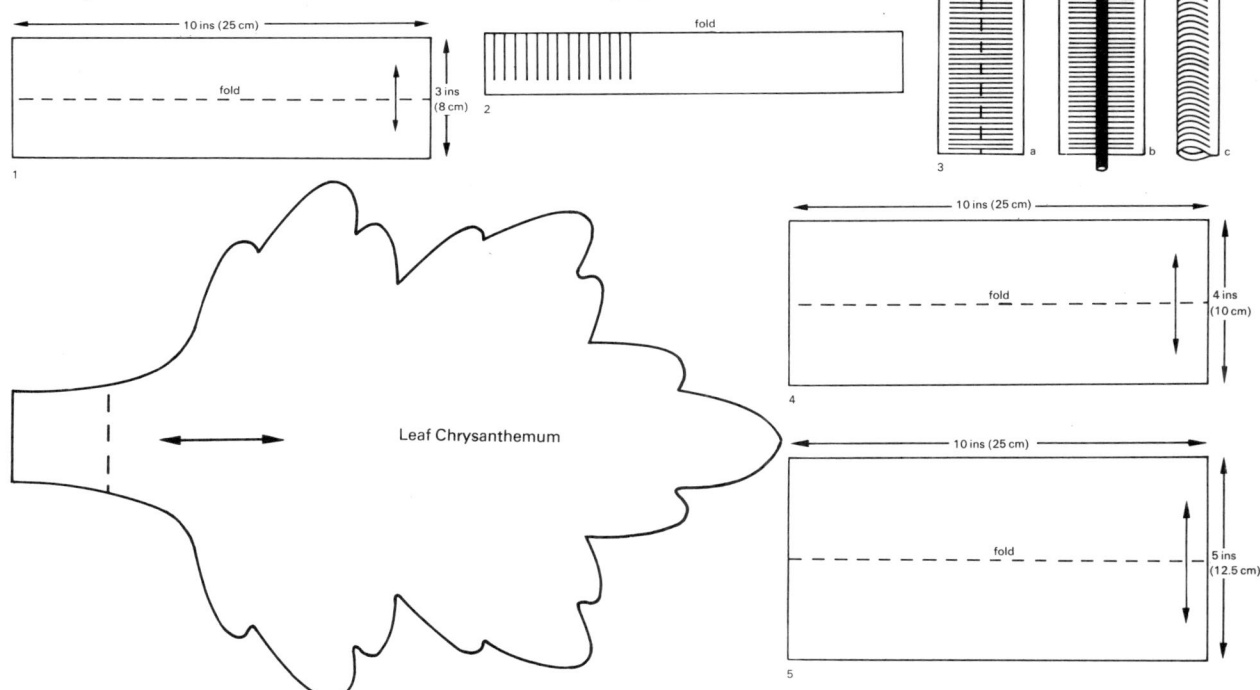

Leaves: Trace the pattern and make a template (page 8). Cut two in green crêpe, and glue round the stem about a third of the way down, opposite each other. Cup slightly (page 8), and lightly stroke the tips (page 8), so that they curl back a little.

Helleborus Niger: Christmas Rose & Ivy

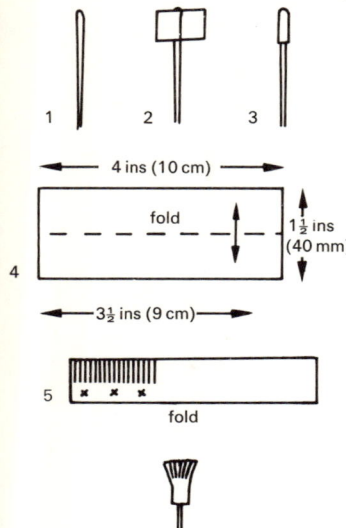

HELLEBORUS NIGER

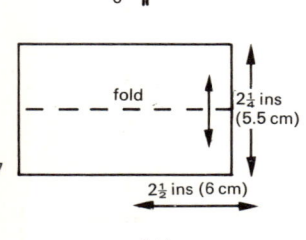

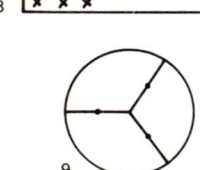

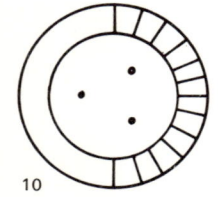

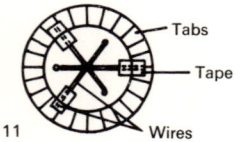

'Helleborus niger *is* the Christmas rose!' you will say. But in this case, there is a distinction: the first is a group of creamy-white flowers, nestling in greenery – the second a glittering confection of gold, pearls and crystal.

Delicate Helleborus Niger

My group suggests the way the flowers nestle together, surrounded by leaves. The single flower and bud decorates a place setting or a gift.

Materials: *White/cream Duplex for petals*
  Deep olive/forest green Duplex crêpe paper for leaves
  Bright and deep yellow crêpe paper for centre
  Olive green crêpe paper for stems (optional)
  Fine soft wire
  Olive green oil crayon, drawing ink or water-colour
  Solid stick adhesive (only if not *using Duplex crêpe)*
  Adhesive tape
  Fabric adhesive or rubber cement
  Stiff card and kitchen foil for flower group
  Soft-ply face tissue
  Plastic-covered garden wire for single flower

Stem and centre: Cut a 7 inch (18 cm) length of fine soft wire. Bend it in half (diagram 1), and thread a 1 inch (25 mm) by ½ inch (10 mm) strip of yellow crêpe paper through the loop (diagram 2): twist and glue the ends tightly round the bent wire (diagram 3).

Cut two pieces of crêpe paper, one each in bright and deep yellow (or both the same) (grain as arrows, diagram 4). Fold each strip in half as indicated and snip the cut edges very closely to a depth of half-way, to form a fine fringe (diagram 5). Glue the two strips lightly together along the folded edge. Then, deeper yellow inside, glue round the covered tip of the stem (diagram 6).

Cut one strip only in bright yellow crêpe as diagram 7. Make a folded fringe strip (page 9) as diagram 8, snipping the *folded* edge very closely to a depth of half-way. Glue this looped fringe round the centre twice, cutting off any excess.

Petals: Trace the pattern (small for group decoration – large for individual flower) and make two templates (page 8). Use one to cut five petals in duplex paper or in the two different crêpes; bond with the paler shade on top.

Mark the second template as indicated by the broken line, and cut away the lower portion. Place over the upper part of a petal, outer edges level; then rub an olive green oil crayon lightly over the uncovered surface of the petal, until you have the depth of colour you require. Smudge softly round the top, to avoid a hard line. Follow the directions for the other Christmas rose.

Cup each petal twice (page 8) – first from the front, fairly fully, just below the centre: then from the back – only slightly this time, just above the centre. Glue the five petals evenly round the centre, each overlapping the previous one. Bind round the base with a narrow strip of crêpe, if necessary.

Sepals: Make a template, and cut two in green duplex or in the two crêpes, bonding these and keeping the lighter shade on top. Cup the centres very fully, and glue them opposite one another, at each side of the flower. Stroke the tips (page 8) so that they curl back slightly.

To make the group decoration: Make three flowers, using the *small* petal pattern. Bind round the base of each with a narrow strip of green crêpe.

Cut a 2½ inch (6 cm) diameter circle of stiff card. Mark the centre, and then rule lines dividing it into three equal (120 degree) sections: mark each line ¾ inch (15 mm) from the outer edge, and make a hole (diagram 9).

Cut a 3½ inch (9 cm) diameter circle of silver foil: place it right side down, and glue the right side of the card to the back, with the foil overlapping all round. Snip this surplus into small tabs (diagram 10), turn them neatly over the edge of the card, and glue to the back. Pierce the foil and thread the stem of a flower through each hole, taping the wire securely to the underside of the card, and cutting off the excess neatly (diagram 11).

Make a template and cut three leaves in duplex or plain crêpes as above, keeping the lighter shade on top; cup the lower half of each. Arrange the flower-heads so that they are angled outwards a little, one sepal on top and the other underneath: glue a leaf between each pair of flowers, as shown.

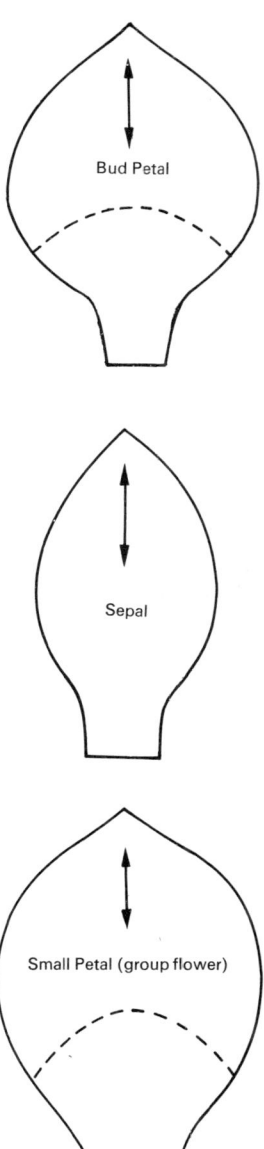

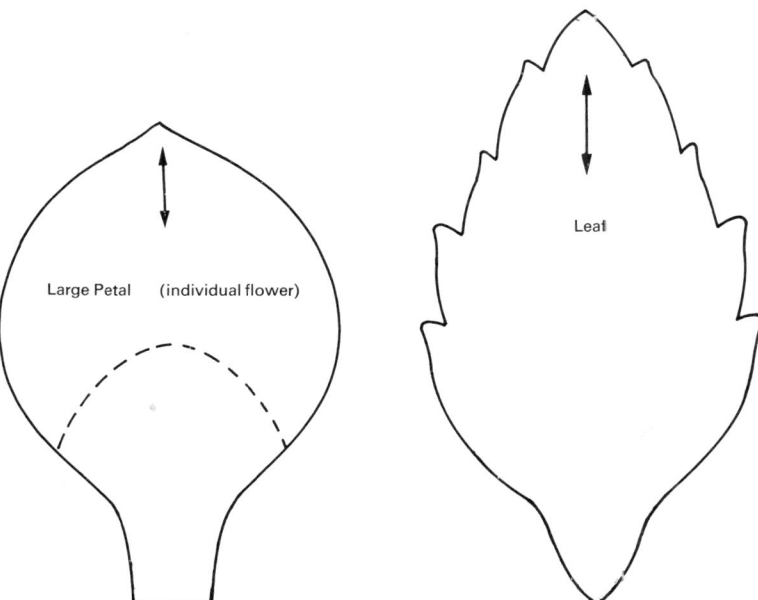

To make the individual flower and bud: Follow the directions above with two exceptions. 1. Cut the longer, looped fringe (diagram 7) 2½ inches (6·5 cm) deep by 3½ inches (9 cm) wide; 2. Use the *larger* petal pattern.

When you have completed the flower-head to the stage shown, cut a piece of garden wire the length you wish your stem to be. Push one end up underneath the flower, tape it neatly to the wire close under the flower and again half-way down and at the bottom of the fine wire. Use narrow strips of face tissue as described on page 10, to pad underneath the centre and form the rounded base of the flower. Then bind the base and stem (page 10).

The bud: Prepare a stem of fine soft wire and make up the first part of the fringed centre following diagrams 1–6 but omitting the looped outer fringe. Using the pattern for the bud petal, cut five and shade the paler side with a light olive tint, as for the flower. This time the deeper shade will be *inside* the flower, so turn the petals over and cup the centres very fully on the deep cream side. Then glue them evenly round the centre, each overlapping the previous one. Cut two sepals, stretch very fully, glue opposite each other, and curl the tips back, as before.

Tape a length of garden wire to the fine wire stem, and pad the base of the bud, as for the flower. Bind the base and half-way down the stem; then place alongside the flower-stem, and continue binding the two together.

Leaf: Make a template, and cut one with the lighter shade on top. Cup the lower half slightly, and stroke the tip to curl it back a little. Glue the base round the double section of stem, just below the point where it divides.

Glittering Christmas Rose

As festive and decorative as gleaming pearls and sparkling crystal can make it!

CHRISTMAS ROSE

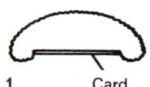

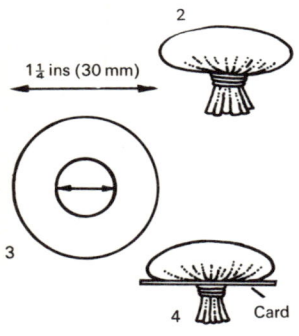

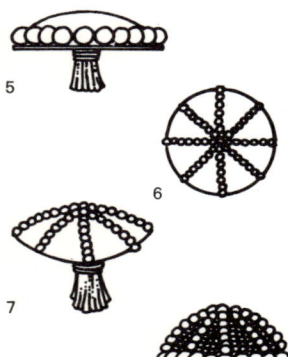

Materials : Creamy-white/deep cream Duplex crêpe paper for petals
Medium-olive/pale olive duplex crêpe paper for leaves
Golden-yellow soft-ply paper for centre
Thin card
Sewing thread or fine wire
Cotton wool
Large pearls, tiny seed pearls and glass beads
Olive green drawing ink or water colour
Solid stick adhesive (only if *not* using Duplex crêpe)
Fabric adhesive or rubber cement
All-purpose clear adhesive (to stick the beads)

Centre: Cut a ¾ inch (20 mm) diameter circle of card. Pad the top with cotton wool, glueing it over the edge of the card (diagram 1).

Cut a 4 inch (10 cm) diameter circle of golden-yellow paper napkins; place over the top of the cotton wool, and draw the edges down smoothly all round. Bind tightly underneath with thread or wire (diagram 2). The diameter should now be just over an inch (25 mm-plus).

Base: Cut a 1¼ inch (30 mm) diameter circle of card, with a ½ inch (10 mm) diameter hole in the middle (diagram 3). Fit the 'tail' of the centre through the hole, so that it sits on top (diagram 4). Thread a circle of large pearls or beads long enough to fit round the centre and rest on the card (diagram 5).

Remove the centre, and decorate with seed pearls, glass beads, or whatever you prefer, or cover it with glitter. I criss-crossed short lengths of tiny seed pearls (diagram 6), glueing them right down over the side, level with the edge of the card (diagram 7). Then I filled in between with tiny glass beads.

Lay a trail of clear adhesive round the outer edge of the base. Press the ring of pearls down on to it, then replace the padded centre to check the position: this should now *sit on top* of the pearl ring – the beads will prevent it fitting inside, as before (diagram 8). Remove the centre again.

Petals: Trace the pattern and make two templates (page 8). Use one to cut fifteen petals with the paler shade on top.

Mark the second template as indicated by the broken line, and cut away the lower portion. Place over the upper part of a petal, outer edges level, and shade the uncovered surface softly with olive drawing ink diluted with a little water as directed on page 10. Tint ten petals, and leave to dry thoroughly.

Cup each petal twice (page 8), first from the front, fairly fully, just below the centre; then from the back, less fully, just above.

Glue five shaded petals evenly round *underneath* the base circle – the lower edges level with the edge of the central hole. Glue five more shaded petals round in the same way, but positioned so that the tips fall exactly *between* the previous petals. Add the remaining plain petals directly behind the first round.

Leaves: Make a template, and cut five with the deeper green on top. Cup each leaf twice, as described for the petal but in reverse, working first from the back and then the front, so that the shaping is in the opposite direction.

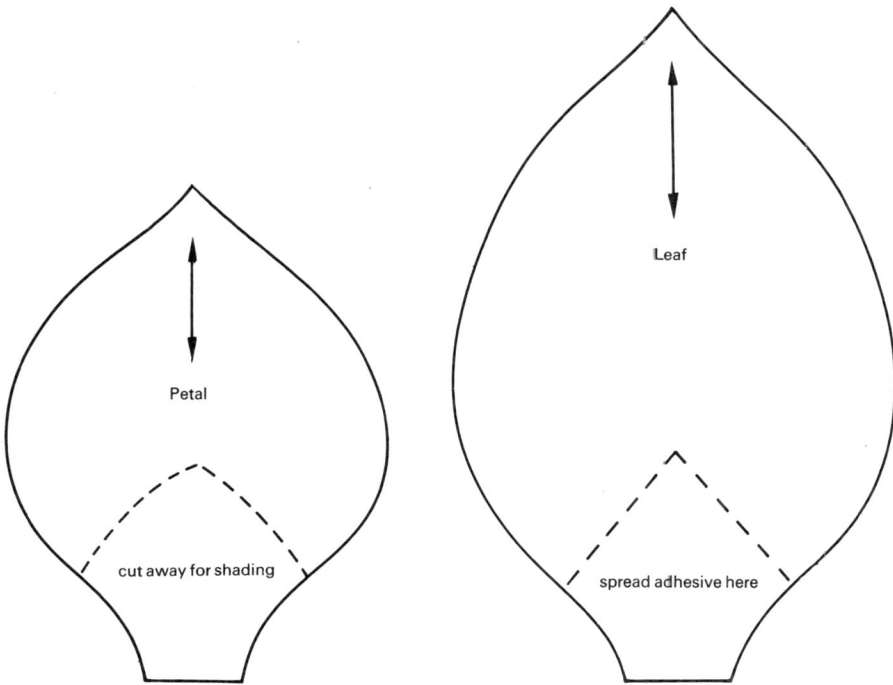

Spread adhesive up to the broken lines, and glue under the base – to fall directly behind the second row of petals.

Replace the centre, making sure it is level – then separate the folds of the 'tail', spread out as flat as possible, and glue smoothly to the card.

Variegated Ivy Trails

To satisfy my passion for ivy, I have designed a trail which can be as long as one likes, can be used singly, or can be joined at the base to resemble a plant.

Materials: *Green/green Duplex crêpe paper for leaves*
Matching or brown single crêpe paper for stems
Fine soft wire
Plastic-covered garden wire
Household bleach (optional)
Solid stick adhesive (only if not using Duplex crêpe)
Fabric adhesive or rubber cement

Variegated Ivy Trails

Leaves: Trace patterns and cut one leaf from each.
Stalks: Cut three pieces of fine soft wire 3 inches (8 cm) long, and four pieces 4 inches (10 cm) long. Bind each very smoothly with single-weight crêpe, as directed on page 10, beginning with a neatly pointed tip (see page 10).

Set the smaller leaf aside. Glue the remaining three small leaves to the shorter stalks, and the four larger leaves to the longer stalks as described on page 11. Place the seven 'stalked' leaves face down on a slightly padded surface; mark veins on the back broken lines following (page 11).

Variegated edges: Dilute a little household bleach with an equal quantity of water. Dip a paint-brush into the solution, and brush it lightly *against the side* of the leaf, so that a little of the bleach is absorbed all round the cut edge:
Stem: Cut a length of garden wire 12–14 inches (30–35 cm) for a single spray, but cut to about 18 inches (45 cm) if you want to join several sprays at the base. Bind the tip as before, continuing on 3 inches (8 cm) down the wire. Glue the smallest leaf to the tip of the stem. Take the next smallest leaf, place the lower half of the stalk alongside the stem, and bind them both securely together (reinforcing the join). About an inch (25 mm) below the point where the second leaf joins the stem, stop again. Align the lower half of the stalk of the next smallest leaf against the *other* side of the stem, and bind the two together as before. Repeat with the next smallest (the fourth) leaf, about an inch (25 mm) below the previous one on the same side as the second leaf.

Continue down the stem, adding the four larger leaves on alternate sides, increasing the distance between them as the leaves grow larger. Bind down to the bottom of the stem, finishing off neatly – or bind in more stems, as required. Arrange the leaves naturally, bending the stem round and curving the centre wires to shape the leaves as illustrated.

Kitchenalia Floribunda

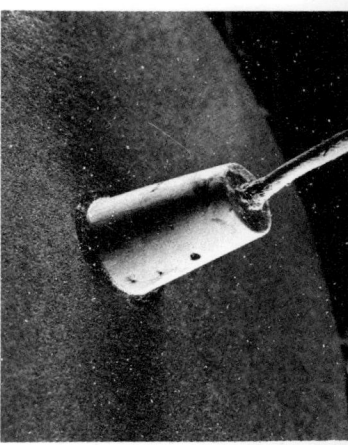

These 'fun flowers' are based on no known species and apart from having stems, centres and petals, might have fallen off the moon! Here are three different varieties, easy to make and using everyday materials.

Many-petalled Pepperella

All you need for these are heavy dark brown and lighter-weight paler brown papers; brown crêpe paper; whole black peppercorns; a small cork, a tiny pin and the usual wires and adhesives.

Trace the flower shape below and cut twice in dark brown paper; then cut a $1\frac{1}{2}$ inch (38 mm) diameter centre circle in the same paper. Using the petal shape only, cut 8 petals in the lighter paper, folding each along the broken line, creasing and unfolding. Run adhesive along each fold, glue four petals to each flower shape and glue the two shapes one over the other, petals alternating.

Push the tip of a length of plastic-covered wire into the cork; bind with brown crêpe (page 10). Glue to the centre back of the flower (see picture) and drive a small pin through the middle of the flower into the cork. Glue peppercorns round the edge of the centre circle and glue it into place.

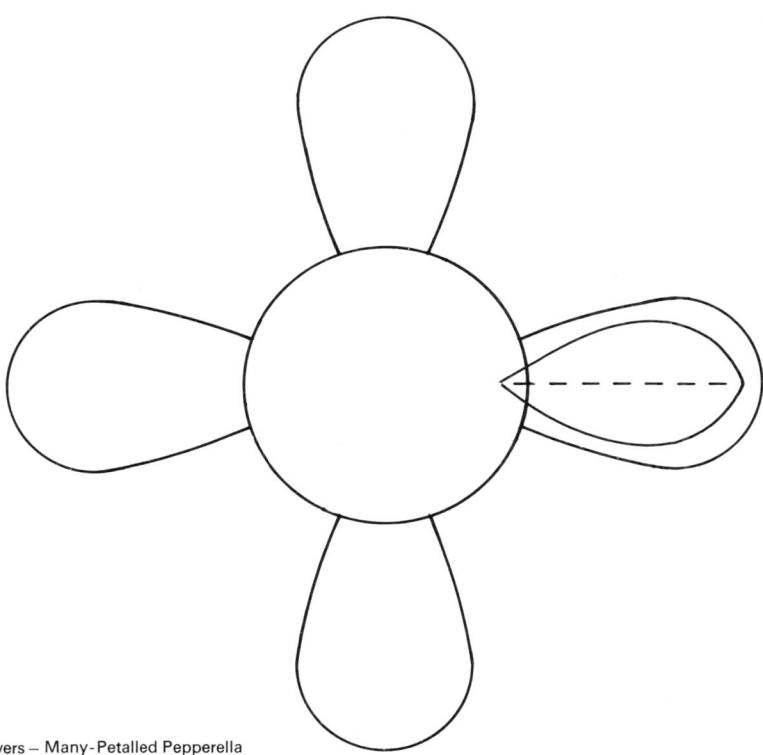

Funflowers – Many-Petalled Pepperella

Coneucopia Parcelis

Brown wrapping paper; brown crêpe paper; sisal string; brown and cream papers and soft yarn for leaves; wires, thread, adhesives – that's all!

Cut plastic-covered wire 1½ inches (40 mm) longer than required length. Bend over 1 inch (25 mm); loop two 4-inch (10 cm) lengths of string through the loops, bind with wire (diagram 1), unravel the string. Cut five 4-inch (10 cm) diameter circles in brown paper; draw a ½-inch (12 mm) circle in the centre of each; divide into equal quarters (diagram 2) cutting out each centre sections (diagram 3). Curve and glue each piece to form a cone – you need nineteen in all. Use one for the centre; glue six more evenly round it, followed by two more rows of six glued between the previous rows. Push the stem down the centre cone; fluff and trim the string and bind the stem with brown crêpe paper (page 10). Trace the leaf pattern a number of times on to the brown and cream papers. Soak a length of yarn in thick wallpaper paste and outline each shape from A to B. When dry, cut round close to the yarn. Bind together three leaf stalks for each flower (see Roses, page 66), glueing leaves in place last. To make the complete plant, bind three leaf stalks to each stem and bind three stems together as for the Roses (page 66).

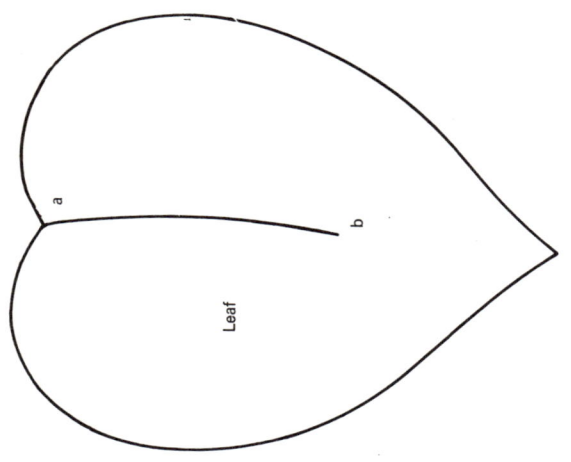

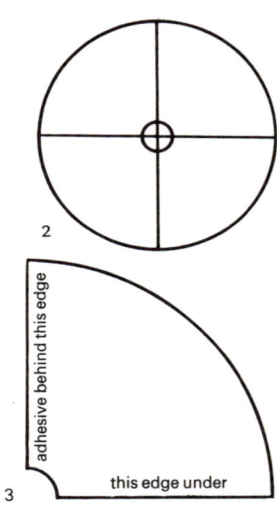

Lentillia Rosetta

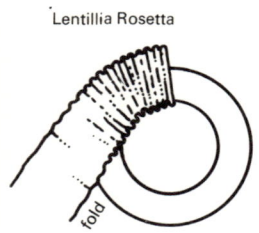

Cream and black papers; brown and black crêpe papers; thin card; lentils and a coffee bean; a cork, a pin, wire and adhesives – and an exotic bloom. Cut two cream circles, one 2-inch (5 cm) and the other 2½-inch (6·5 cm) diameter. Glue a slightly smaller card circle behind the first and draw a 1½-inch (40 cm) diameter circle in the centre of the second. Glue lentils round the edge of the smaller circle, a coffee bean and more lentils in the centre. Cut an 18 × 1½-inch (4·5 × 4 cm) length of brown crêpe, grain running widthways; fold in half across the grain. Frill long cut edges (page 8), gather the folded edge tightly and glue evenly against the edge of the marked line on the larger circle. Cut a 3½-inch (9 cm) diameter black paper circle; draw a 2½-inch (6·5 cm) circle in the centre. Cut a 24 × 1½-inch (6 × 4 cm) strip of black crêpe; make up and glue to the circle as above. Glue the brown circle over the black one. Make the cork and wire stem and fix as for the Pepperella. Glue the centre in place.

Moonbeam Icicalia

An ethereal decoration to entrance your Christmas callers on the kind of frosty night which inspired it. Change the blues to a delicate pink for a wedding reception. Use gold to celebrate a golden wedding anniversary. As a sophisticated arrangement choose a rich plum or aubergine, or bitter chocolate with bleached grass and gold leaves.

Materials: White buckram or stiff paper for the flowers
Silver/blue metallic paper or foil for the leaves
Medium or pale blue crêpe paper for sepals and stems
Blue fluffy dried grass
Pearl beads in four sizes and tiny glass beads
Sewing thread : Fine soft wire
Transparent adhesive tape and adhesives

Flower: Trace the three sizes – A, B and C – and make individual templates (page 8). Cut each once in buckram or paper. Curve the straight lower edge of each flower round, overlapping corners x, and either catch them neatly together with two or three stitches, or glue them, leaving a narrow, funnel-shaped hole (diagram 1).

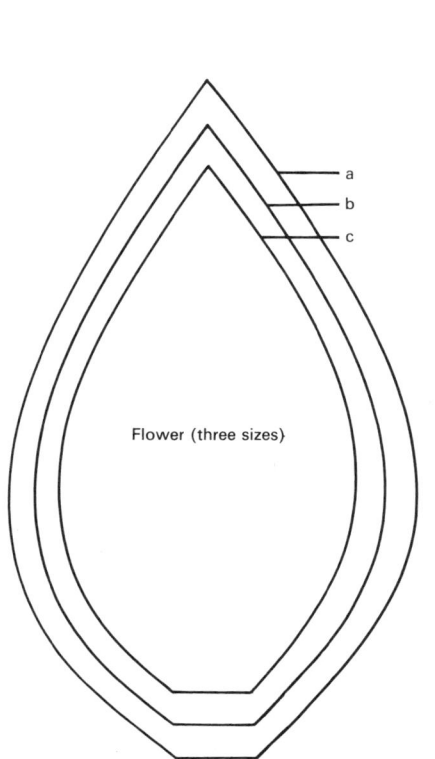

Flower (three sizes)

a
b
c

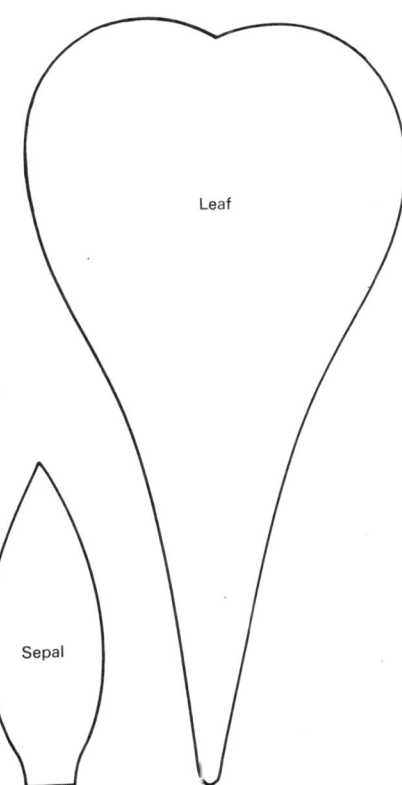

Leaf

Sepal

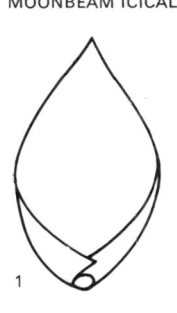

MOONBEAM ICICALIA

1

93

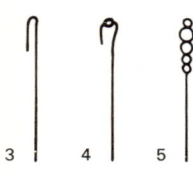

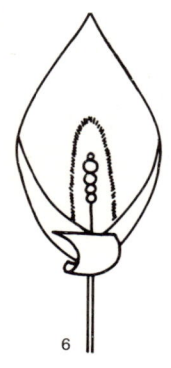

Sepals: Make a template, and cut three in medium blue crêpe. Stroke to curl them (page 8); then glue one across the front of each flower, over the stitches, as illustrated.

Centre: Lower the stalk of a grass-head through each hole, so that the head rests inside the flower (diagram 2).

To make up a spray, you will need four pieces of fine soft wire which are basically 12 inches (30 cm), 10 inches (25 cm), 8 inches (20 cm) and 6 inches (15 cm) long, when they are to carry a flower only. However, add 3 inches (7 cm) to the wire on which you plan to have the leaf. Thus, for a leaf at the base, cut the final wire 9 inches (22 cm) long.

Bend back the tip of each *flower* wire about $\frac{1}{2}$ inch (10 mm) (diagram 3), catching a tiny clear glass bead (if you have one) in the loop (diagram 4). Then thread four pearls in graduated sizes up the wire, right under the loop (diagram 5). Twist a small blob of clear adhesive round the wire, close under the smallest pearl; leave to dry.

Lower the longest wire through the hole in the largest flower (A) in front of the grass-head, so that the pearl tip is half the height of the grass-head (see diagram 6 and picture).

Stem: Bind the wire and grass-stalk tightly together with pale blue crêpe, as directed on page 10.

Repeat with flower B and the 10 inch (25 cm) wire; begin to bind the stem but pause 2 inches (5 cm) below the base of the flower, and place alongside the bound stem of the previous one at a point 4 inches (10 cm) below the base of flower A. Bind securely together. Repeat with flower C and the 8 inch (20 cm) wire, binding it to the main stem 2 inches (5 cm) below the previous join and on the opposite side from flower B.

Leaf: Make a template, and cut once in metallic paper or foil.

Fix the 9 inch (22 cm) wire to the underside of the leaf with transparent tape, as diagram 7.

Bind the leaf-stalk and join to the main stem as before, 2 inches (5 cm) below the previous join and on the opposite side from flower C, below B.

Curve the pearl centres outwards slightly, as illustrated, and bend the central wire to shape the leaf.

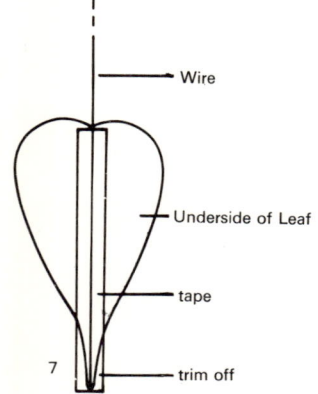

For the decoration illustrated on page 80, I made two sprays with the leaf at the base – and then three more with leaves in different positions, substituting the leaf for a flower at the required height and binding in the remaining flowers below. Adjust the stem measurements accordingly.

Each spray consists of three graduated flowers and one leaf.

Glossary of Equivalents

Buff manilla paper thin brown paper with rag-weave texture
Cartridge paper construction paper
Cocktail stick large toothpick or manicure stick
Concertina-wise accordian folds
Cotton wool cotton balls, cotton batting
Drawing ink water-color paint or water-based ink
Fabric adhesive craft glue such as Sobo
Fine soft wire craft wire
Greaseproof paper tracing paper
Parcel wrapping paper thin brown wrapping paper
Silver (kitchen) foil aluminum foil
Silver/blue metallic paper florists foil paper
Soft-ply tissue 4-ply facial tissue or very soft napkin
Thin card lightweight cardboard
Tiny pin $\frac{5}{8}$ inch straight pin

Index

Adhesives 7
Adhesive tape 7
African marigolds 28
Anemones 22
Asters 41
Attaching leaves 11

Basic methods 8
Binding 10
Bonding crêpe paper 9
Buttercups 12

Cabbage rose 71
Canterbury bells 49
Carnations 39
Centres 10
Champs Elysees rose 65
Christmas rose 86, 88
Chrysanthemum 84
Classic roses 63
Colouring crêpe paper 10
Colour-shaded dahlias 83
'Coneucopia parcelis' 92
Cornflowers 61
Covering centres 10
Crêpe paper 6
   Water painting 11
Cupping 8
Curling 8
Cutting petals and leaves 8
Cutting double petals and leaves 9

Daffodils 15
Dahlias 83
Daisies 13
Double chrysanthemums 84
Duplex crêpe paper 6

Equipment 7

Fabric adhesive 7
Feathery Love-in-a-Mist 37
Field Buttercups 12
   Cornflowers 61
   Poppies 59

Fixing fringe and petals 9
Floribunda rose spray 73
Flowers and stems 9
Folded fringe 9
French marigold 26
Frilling 8
Frilly Pincushion flowers 55
Fringe, folded 9
   fixing 9
   speedy snipping 9

Gentians 19
Glittering Christmas rose 88

Helleborus niger 86

Ivy trails 89

Jagged edges 11
Japanese anemone 22

'Kitchenalia Floribunda' 91

Leaves 11
   attaching to stalks 11
   cutting (double) 9
   cutting (single) 8
   jagged edges 11
   veins 11

Making up double petals and leaves 9
Many-petalled peony 81
   pepperella 91
Marigolds 26
Materials 6
Matterhorn rose 65
Meadow daisies 13
Metric measurements 7
Moonbeam icicalia 93
Morning glory 30
Moss roses 33
Mountain gentians 19

Narcissus 19

Painting 11

Padding 10
   stems 10
Papers 6
Peony 81
Petals, cutting 8, 9
   fixing 9
   shaping 8
Petunia 53
Pincushion flowers 55
Plain tissue paper 6
Poet's narcissus 19
Poppies 59
Prize asters 41
   carnations 39

Radiant sunflower 76
Ranunculus 51
Roses 63–75

St Brigid anemone 23
Scarlet poppies 59
Soft-ply tissue 6
Solid stick adhesive 7
Speedy fringe snipping 9
Stems 6, 9, 10, 11
Stroking 8
Sunflower 76

Tape, adhesive 7
Techniques 8
Templates 8
Tiger lilies 43
Tips of stalks 10
Tissues 6
Trailing morning glory 3
Trumpet daffodils 15

Variegated ivy 89
Veins 11
Vienna Charm rose 66

Water-painting crêpe 11
Wires and stems 6